advance praise

"A Godsend for all those moving through the transition of divorce. This is a heartfelt and humane guide to healing through divorce, written with love and compassion."

Mel Schwartz C.S.W.
Psychotherapist and author of
The Art of Intimacy, *The Pleasure of Passion*

"Micki McWade has written a powerful, straight-forward book which should prove to be an invaluable guide to those in divorce recovery and those wanting to start a group of their own. *Getting Up, Getting Over, Getting On* is an easy-to-read book in which the 12-steps are artfully applied to divorce recovery. The exercises are well designed and the reader will find the first-hand accounts of group members especially helpful."

Pamela D. Blair, Psychotherapist & Director
Divorce Resource Network
Publisher, *Surviving Divorce* newsletter
Contributing Editor, *Divorce NY/NJ Magazine*

"Micki McWade offers a practical guide through the treacherous terrain of divorce and its aftermath. Her book, a comprehensive resource and easily accessible companion for anyone going through divorce, provides the essential tools for building a new and better life. It should be required reading for all matrimonial attorneys and those whom they represent. I have read the book, I have attended the Recovery Group meetings and I have seen Micki McWade's tips and techniques work to bring those caught in the quagmire of divorce to a successful recovery—step by step."

Stephen G. Gordon, Esq.

"Micki McWade artfully combines her experience, clear thinking, gentle humor and compassion with grace and creates the possibility of healing. I highly recommend you accept her invitation to recovery."

Linda Seaver, MPS, ATR

"From the very first word, Micki McWade's warmth and wisdom reach past pain to provide comfort and clarity. As she walks beside the reader, telling her own story along the way, she guides one, unerringly, through the turmoil and grief that accompany divorce, to self-empowerment and peace. With straight-forward good sense she maps a clear and inviting path to recovery 'one step at a time.'"

Barbara Marantz, Ph.D.

Psychologist

"The 12 Steps and the power of the group allowed me to grow through a separation I neither wanted nor expected. Yes grow through, not go through. That growth and the tools for living the program provides are now helping me try to restore my marriage. Whether or not my husband and I succeed, the steps and the friendships I made in the group have given me the foundation for building a happier life."

Karla F.

Group Member

Getting Up
Getting Over
Getting On

A Twelve Step Guide
to Divorce Recovery

Getting Up
Getting Over
Getting On

A Twelve Step Guide
to Divorce Recovery

Micki McWade

CHAMPION PRESS, LTD.
BEVERLY HILLS

Acknowledgment
The prayer that appears on page 25 is used with permission. From
ILLUMINATA by Marianne Williamson
Copyright © 1995 by Marianne Williamson. Reprinted by permission of Random
House, Inc.

CHAMPION PRESS, LTD.
BEVERLY HILLS, CALIFORNIA

Library of Congress Catalog Card Number 98-074569

ISBN 1-891400-13-4

Cataloging-in-Publication Data

McWade, Micki.
    Getting up, getting over, getting on : a twelve step guide to divorce recovery /
Micki McWade. —
1st ed.
        p. cm.
    Includes bibliographical references and index
    LCCN: 98-74569
    ISBN: 1-891400-13-4

    1. Divorce—Psychological aspects 2. Twelve-step programs. I Title.

HQ814.M39 1999   306.89
                                        QP199-49

Manufactured in the United States of America
10 9 8 7 6 5 4 3 2 1

Book Design by Pilot Publishing, Milwaukee, Wisconsin

With love to Meredith, Charlie, Megan and Joe
who walked the path with me.

Acknowledgments

I'm grateful to my Higher Power for the inspiration and continued support to write this book. I want to thank the women and men of Al-Anon who were my teachers and inspiration.

Thanks go to Elizabeth S., who was with me since the conception of our Divorce Recovery group, and who remains a constant support, friend and co-leader. To Sally F. who is always willing to lend a hand and has provided inspiration for many others who have come later.

Thanks to Risa Tabacoff, my therapist, who has been a valuable guide and healer to my family and me.

Thanks to all the members, past and present, of the St. Mark's Wednesday night meeting of the Twelve Step Separation/Divorce Recovery Group who have generously shared their insights, understanding and growth.

To my friend Joan Guthrie, who walked with me every day and listened, encouraged and supported me through the darkest times.

I am grateful to my mentors—Barbara Gordon and Barbara Marantz, for their support and to Thelma Jurgrau, my teacher at Empire State College, State University of New York, for her suggestions and encouragement on this project.

Love and thanks to Gary Ditlow for his support and belief in my ability to write this book.

Thanks to Chuck McWade, who never missed a support payment and provided financial stability so that, along with my job, I could return to school and have the peace of mind to write.

Thanks to Gene Krackehl who encouraged me from the beginning and for his advice on the book design.

Thanks and admiration go to my editor, Brook Noel, whose expertise and flexibility made the process seem non-threatening and feel like fun—not an easy job.

I wish to express appreciation to Pam Blair for her workshops, newsletters and continued support of the group. And to Melody Beattie for her book *The Language of Letting Go*, which has provided an important source of comfort and wisdom for both myself and many members of our group.

Contents

Section Two
ℭ Tools for Recovery ℬ

Chapter Four

Chapter Five

Chapter Six

Chapter Seven

Introduction

In the fall of 1990, I was feeling more fear than I had felt in my entire life. My husband and I were separating after 23 years—our whole adult lives. We had four children, a house, a dog and a cat. I had not worked full time since the children were born.

Before we were married, because of family illness, I lived at home with my mother. I hadn't gone away to college or lived on my own. Now I would be the only adult in the house and would be parenting four adolescents alone.

Aside from parental worries, I was almost paralyzed with fear about money. I was aware of how much one needed to keep a house going and provide for children. I knew I couldn't do it by myself. What if he took off? What if he didn't help me? Everyone had a horror story. "You better get a good lawyer!" they said.

I remember going to the supermarket the day after my husband moved out and crying over the tomatoes. His favorite dinner was steak and salad, so I had cut up many a tomato in our time together. Memories flooded my mind and the grief was overwhelming. The marriage had been troubled for a long time but the breakup was far worse than I had anticipated.

Fortunately, at that time, I was a member of Al-Anon (a support group for families of alcoholics) and practicing the Twelve Steps. The Steps had a way of clarifying confusion, reducing turmoil and creating peace—albeit briefly in the beginning. When I awoke in the middle of the night with a feeling of dread, the Serenity Prayer allowed me to go back to sleep. When I got steamed up about what someone said or did, Step One reminded me about self-responsibility.

Spending time in an Al-Anon group inspired me to start a support group for separated and divorced people. I didn't want to be with anyone who would exacerbate my fear, whip up my hostility or increase my bitterness. I needed to be with people who understood that self-pity and blame would make things worse. I needed friends who were learning to be self-directed and self-reliant, so I invited separated and divorced Al-Anon people, and a few others who were interested in pursuing growth through this nightmare, to join me in a new Twelve Step meeting. On September 8, 1993, the Separation/Divorce Recovery Group was formed and on our fifth anniversary we had 65 members.

Friends and neighbors were surprised to see how well our divorce went. We helped each other when we could and avoided scenes. Our children went through some difficult times, but they are doing well today.

This book contains tools for your recovery tool bag. These ideas are helpful during the time of divorce and in constructing the rest your life as you go forward. They apply in the workplace, in relationships with children, with in-laws and (ex)spouses.

I hope that you will decide to find a group or start your own group of divorcing people to work with. Through shared experience you will gain the wisdom to handle your own situation with grace, dignity and peace.

My hope for you is that you will find strength and comfort within these Steps. They offer practical suggestions for getting through the tumult and minimizing long-term damage to you and your family. I wrote this book to tell you that you *will* survive a divorce. Not only will you survive, you will see that divorce is a gateway into your own potential.

Chapter One

Understanding Divorce and the Road to Recovery

It's no revelation that divorce is a traumatic event. Divorce deeply affects the individual who makes the decision and, of course, his or her spouse. The effects also radiate out into a much wider circle. First, divorce affects and traumatizes everyone in the immediate family; then it affects the couple's extended family and friends to varying degrees.

Divorce produces fear in all parties involved—the couple, their children, parents, siblings, friends. Fear of change and fear of abandonment are present in everyone, at least some of the time. We get angry about facing that fear. Sometimes friends or family members avoid or reject us because we make them feel uncomfortable. So divorce can be an isolating experience.

The changes that divorce precipitate only increase the feeling of isolation. We're moving from the married to the unmarried state. The people we live with change. The attitudes of the people we live with change. Relatives and friends that were related to our partner's life may no longer be present. Where we live might change. Having less money is normal in this situation.

There is grieving to be done and there are many losses. We grieve for the death of a relationship, a dream, a lifestyle, of what we know as normal. We grieve for our children's losses, and even for our pets.

Often when we are in pain we stay home and hibernate. We feel unattractive, unwanted, vulnerable. It seems like everything we are experiencing on the inside is obvious to everyone on the outside. Isolation is not good for most of us, who by nature are sociable. During the process of separation and divorce, the need for connection is stronger than usual because of the losses in other areas. Some of our friends may be taking sides, or feel that we are overloading them on the subject. We may no longer feel comfortable talking to the people we have talked to in the past. We need to be with people who understand. This doesn't mean we can't stay connected to our friends from the past, but it's constructive to seek out people who can relate to us in the new situation as well.

Change is the key word in divorce. Unexpected change is more painful than change we plan for. If we are part of a support group, we find people who also have been through this experience and some who are presently living through this experience. While no two situations are exactly the same, it's helpful to hear solutions and reassurances from others who have survived the process and have learned something along the way. Personal growth, survival tips and compassionate company are often the by-products of meeting in a group.

Whether we were the one who wanted to leave the marriage or the one who was left, so much seems out of our control. We may feel a combination of any of the following: fear, abandonment, rejection, hurt, humiliation, self-centeredness, self-doubt, self-absorption, anger, depression, misery. And we may believe that we'll never be happy again.

These feelings, and the ramifications of the situation itself, are similar to those of people recovering from alcohol or drug abuse and of their families. The helplessness, hopelessness, fear of change, obsessiveness about another person's behavior and being unable to rely on anything or anyone except ourselves are like the feelings in other recovery situations.

There are two parts to a proven formula for getting our lives together. One is to practice the Twelve Steps of AA and Al-Anon. Why? Because they have been helping people for more than 50 years—encouraging us to focus on ourselves and our own behavior—to discover what we did to wind up in this place at this time. We take our share of the responsibility (large or small) and seek to understand ourselves so we don't continue to make the same mistakes over and over.

The other is belonging to a support group. Joining a group has proven effective in recovery from cancer, heart attacks, alcoholism, drug addiction, eating too much, the loss of a child and the loss of a spouse. Why is it so effective? Because we understand each other. We have patience to listen. We learn from each other. We establish new friendships.

We learn that there's help to be found in many ways. If we're lucky enough to find a divorce support group, we realize that we aren't alone. In a Twelve Step support group we listen to others speak at meetings and we come to realize that we too have a Higher Power.

It is natural and necessary for us to focus on the past—to think about what happened and why. We have to deal with our own pain, our children's pain, our family's and friends' reactions, the legal process and our (ex)spouse, but there has to be, and is, more to life than pain, grief and aggravation. This will become apparent as we move through the process.

Believe it or not, divorce can be a gateway to a new life. So many opportunities for change occur during this process. We can use these opportunities to create wonderful new things if we don't stay in the "victim" role. It is up to us to spend our energy choosing wisely and creatively. We want to be proactive in our recovery.

Vision is greater than baggage.
—*Stephen R. Covey*

The Twelve Steps help us focus on *ourselves*—what is right and good in us, and in a gentle way, on our shortcomings. The Steps invoke the loving support of whatever Higher Power we can imagine, and they show us the process by which we can be and feel lovable. We can learn, practice and share our experience in a group.

Belonging to a group is good because divorce is lonely. We need people in our lives, but it can be a strong temptation to pick up the pieces with someone else, as part of a new couple, too soon. We need to complete ourselves (or recover) by ourselves first. Joining a support group connects us with other people without having to make the couple-connection.

The process of divorce is like having a leg amputated. We are in a lot of pain, we miss it terribly even though it may have hurt a great deal before, and we are definitely off balance. The first impulse may be to replace it as fast as possible; to grab a new leg and make it work—no compatibility test or size consideration, no waiting for some healing to take place. We panic. We think "I *can't walk* with just one leg!" Just hide the wound and act normal. We tell ourselves "I'm OK, I'm OK, I'll be fine." We'll do anything to make that feeling of loss go away.

The problem with acting too soon is that we probably won't pick the right replacement and will later face another "rejection." Healing will be superficial, and the infection from the first wound may undermine the new attachment.

We need TIME to heal. It's true that we can't walk with one leg, but there are aids for us to use until we heal—therapy, wheelchairs, crutches, medications, etc. Immediately after a serious injury or major illness we feel really weak, have pain and get discouraged. We may feel that it will always be like this. We feel depressed, exhausted, wanting to pull the covers up over our heads and just stay in bed. After a while though, our perspective changes and we realize that we feel better. The pain has lessened and we have more energy.

Divorce is even more than an external trauma—it's an illness of the emotions and the psyche. It too needs recovery time. The length of the healing period differs for everyone, so we need to respect our own recovery process and give ourselves the time we need to heal. The first year is the most difficult.

Twelve Step groups, meditation, getting in touch with nature, developing new friendships and individual therapy are some of the aids available to help us heal from the trauma of divorce.

After doing the work on ourselves, we slowly regain balance. This kind of balance won't be undermined. We create our own foundation, growing stronger than we were before. This process encourages us to go forward in our lives one day at a time.

Pushing ourselves to grow and change, rather than feeling sorry for ourselves and stagnating, is harder to do initially, but it's an investment in the future. We can learn a lot about ourselves when we go through a divorce and if we do, we may avoid repeating self-defeating behavior. We don't want to go through this again! *The work is worth it!*

> *Until a person can say deeply and honestly, 'I am what I am today because of the choices I made yesterday,' that person cannot say 'I choose otherwise.'*
> —Stephen R. Covey

Creating or re-creating ourselves as individuals and assessing our needs NOW are of critical importance. To accept the same criteria we set up before marriage would be a big mistake. We are no longer the same person.

We can ask ourselves what we want to do with our lives in the new context. What interests us? Whom do we want to spend time with? What activities make us happy? What kind of vacation would we enjoy? Perhaps we should think about more education. There's a lot of freedom at this point. It's up to us to choose *good* things for ourselves.

Spirituality

The relationship with a Higher Power is an individual one. Some of us call our Higher Power God; some, the Universe; others believe in angels, and the list can go on and on. Some of us use the power present in the group as our Higher Power. The love, support, strength and healing found in the recovery work and the relationships established within the group are evident and powerful.

Many people have a problem with the idea of a Higher Power. Some of us have rejected the religious practices that we learned as children. Others were never taught any religious traditions. Some of us have experienced rejection from those traditions for various reasons, including divorce. Some of us have strong religious beliefs and find the support of religion and its community to be invaluable.

It may be helpful to remember that the idea of a Higher Power is bigger than any one religion. Religious practices are not God, only avenues to God, and we don't have to be religious to have contact with our Higher Power. We just have to ask and be open to the possibilities.

The main idea is to realize that there's more out there than just us. We don't have to know all the answers today. I believe we are being cared for and watched over whether we realize it or not. We just have to be willing to allow our Higher Power to enter our lives. God, or the Higher Power in any form, responds to invitation.

Being in touch with our Higher Power reduces fear and can pull us out of a funk. We may realize that the sun still shines, we are alive, there are people we can relate to and that joy is possible. Even in periods of sadness, we can still enjoy the beauty of nature, the perfume of flowers, the smile of a child, the hug of a friend, the taste of a favorite food, the distraction of an entertaining movie. While we remain in fear, we see only darkness. Our whole point of view is skewed. We may believe that we'll never feel better or be like our old selves again. Fear is very debilitating.

When we're in touch with our Higher Power—which can be done by prayer, meditation, attending meetings, going to church, taking a walk, reading uplifting material—the fear dissolves and we can be good for ourselves, for our children and for anyone with whom we come in contact.

The Serenity Prayer

God, grant me the serenity
to accept the things I cannot change,
the courage to change the things I can
and the wisdom to know the difference.

Twelve Step groups of all kinds use the Serenity Prayer to invoke our Higher Power to help us sort out issues in our lives that are causing pain and stress. Those of us who deal with the problems of divorce can easily relate to the things we can and cannot change and the need for serenity.

From this realization growth begins because with time and practice we learn to spend our energy only on circumstances that are within our power to change. We become less overwhelmed, depressed, anxious and frustrated. The reward is feeling more composed, creative, peaceful and in charge of our lives.

When I began the Twelve Step practice in Al-Anon ten years ago, I didn't have a strong relationship with God. I had had religious training as a child, but I found the focus on formalized prayer and on rules and regulations distracting so I decided to talk to God in my own way. However, I didn't do it very often. In the last ten years my relationship with God has expanded dramatically. In Twelve Step meetings I heard many stories of prayers being answered. Ordinary people were telling them—people with shortcomings, fears, and doubts about life and God. They were not priests, ministers or rabbis, but they spoke of miracles nevertheless.

My awakening started by hearing their stories. I began to ask "Why not me? I sure could use some miracles at this point in my life. "

I used to wake up feeling fearful, with a case of the "What ifs?" I've also heard this referred to as "awful-izing." I thought of all the bad scenarios possible with regard to the house, my kids, the dog, my health, my finances, the car and so forth. I was miserable and decided I had nothing to lose by putting into practice what I had learned. So before I got out of bed in the morning, I began to invite God into my life for the day. This felt good, and it couldn't hurt me, right? I didn't feel quite so alone. A glimmer of hope was visible. I read that God enters by invitation, not by force.

The days I asked for help went smoother. I got to places on time. The computer worked. I was able to concentrate better. The lines in the supermarket were shorter. Someone called to tell me about a course being offered or about some other good thing, or just to say hello. I got the job I wanted.

My faith grew as I realized that my life was working well and that when I asked for help, it came. It's not that things never went wrong, but solutions became apparent. I coped without panic and saved a lot of time.

For example, my daughter called me from college to tell me she was in the emergency room. The diagnosis was possible appendicitis. She was very sick and frightened. It was 11:30 p.m. and the hospital was a 150 miles away, in the middle of an unfamiliar city. I wanted to go, but I would have to go alone.

I asked my Higher Power for help for Megan and guidance for me and prepared to leave my house. I arrived at the hospital in the nick of time at 2:00 a.m. The emergency room nurse rushed me to where Megan was waiting on a gurney just outside of the operating room. I was able to talk with her before she went into surgery and assure her that she would be fine. She said later that she felt safe knowing I was there.

Megan came through very well, recovering quickly. I was well taken care of, too. The operation took less time than I expected so I wasn't overly worried. There was a comfortable chair next to her bed so I could be with her and still get some rest. My boss gave me three days off with pay, and when Megan's dad visited, he told me he'd pay the rest of my car loan.

You could call all of this coincidence, but I know better, and I am very grateful.

In time, the practice of the Twelve Steps will bring balance, maturity, serenity, self-knowledge and forgiveness into our lives. It can change the quality of our lives, as well as the quality of the people we attract. We can learn to stop attracting the same harmful situation over and over again. Thousands of people have already made these changes in their lives.

Chapter Two

Exploring the Twelve Step Recovery Program

My Twelve Step journey began in 1989, when my brother-in-law entered the hospital for the second time, suffering from cirrhosis of the liver. He was yellow, swollen and talking nonsense because his brain chemistry had been altered by his steady consumption of alcohol. I couldn't believe that he had done this again after being told he would die if he continued to drink.

So much of my life had been affected by other family members' drinking habits and at that moment, I felt rage and frustration toward them all. I took the advice of a good friend who was a member of Alcoholics Anonymous and went to an Al-Anon meeting. (Al-Anon is a support group for families and friends of alcoholics.) Joe died four months later at the age of forty-nine.

In Al-Anon I learned that I wasn't alone with these feelings and that there was a great deal to be learned about the disease of alcoholism. Not only did this disease drastically affect the drinker, but it had definite and predictable effects on the family and friends of the drinker. Alcoholism affects families so significantly that there are three large national groups—Al-Anon, Al-Ateen and Adult Children of Alcoholics (ACOA) to help people cope with this disease.

During my five-year education in the groups I learned that I didn't have to stand for being manipulated by others;

that I was responsible for my own behavior, regardless of what other people did; that I couldn't change other people's behavior no matter how good or smart I was or how rational an argument I presented; and that I'd wasted enough time and energy focusing on events over which I had no control.

I learned that I had plenty of power in my own life, and changing my life for the better was entirely possible. Many of my personal limitations were self-created. I learned that a Higher Power was available to me. One could ask for help and receive it. Inner guidance was available, and the right answers would come if I was quiet enough to hear them. As a child, I was taught that God had a lot of rules and that I wasn't worthy of His grace if they weren't followed. In the Al-Anon rooms people told wonderful stories of receiving strength and healing by making direct requests and doing so without worry or guilt.

For the first time in my life I was clear about what my responsibility was and what it was that I owed to others. For example, as a mother I needed to take care of the children—but I deserved a day off and some rest occasionally. As a wife, I had to take care of certain responsibilities—but when the baby was sick and I could not get all the errands done, it was all right to let them go for a while. If family members drank to excess and avoided responsibilities, I could say what I thought—but I couldn't expect them to change because I said so. I could choose to live with it, or not—that was my choice.

When it became obvious that a divorce was inevitable I began to apply my Al-Anon program to my divorce proceedings. I was grateful to have had this program experience before my divorce because it saved the family a lot of pain. I found that my behavior influenced my husband—for better and worse. If I behaved sanely, so did he. If I lost control, so did he. If he got angry, I didn't have to get angry too. I could *choose* my reaction. I did the best I could, turned the rest over to my Higher Power for the best solution possible, and focused on myself and my own responsibilities.

Because I was an Al-Anon member, I had support from people who were also clear-thinking. There were people available to have dinner or go to the movies with me. I could talk things over and mourn my loss, but I didn't feel lost or alone all the time. I had my Higher Power and my Al-Anon friends to support me. Because I didn't feel isolated, I didn't often succumb to the fear and suspicion that can be magnified by being alone too much.

I knew from experience how valuable the Twelve Steps were. I knew that many people had been helped by this process. I learned that the use of the Twelve Steps is the most successful long-term treatment of alcoholism and other addictive behaviors. Why do the Twelve Steps apply to divorce, which, unlike alcoholism, is not a problem of addiction? Because when we take something important out of our lives, it leaves a large hole. It's in our nature to fill that void as quickly as possible, and what we do at that time may not be in our own best interest. Confusion may reign for a while. We struggle to make sense of the new context and to redefine our new perspective.

Here is some of what I learned in Al-Anon that is useful with divorce:

Take one day at a time, especially in the early stages.

I am responsible for my own behavior. I cannot control what others may or may not do. If I monitor my own behavior and take care of my responsibilities I will have less to worry about and to apologize for.

Change creates fear—whether you're giving up alcohol and the friends associated with drinking, or you're giving up the lifestyle that you knew with your spouse—fear of the unknown is present in both scenarios. We all ask ourselves "What's to become of me? How will I survive in the new circumstances? Will I be able to make the adjustment?"

With the end of alcoholism, or joining an Al-Anon group, we may see ourselves clearly for the first time in years and know that changes have to be made. With divorce much change is demanded and we too have to seek out new people who will support and encourage us as we go forward into our new lives.

The Steps are a system of behavior that facilitates change, that gets us off on the right foot. They teach us to make global personality changes—not just to deal with a specific problem.

The Twelve Steps of Alcoholics Anonymous

---

1. We admitted we were powerless over alcohol—that our lives had become unmanageable.

2. Came to believe that a Power greater than ourselves could restore us to sanity.

3. Made a decision to turn our will and our lives over to the care of God, *as we understood Him.*

4. Made a searching and fearless moral inventory of ourselves.

5. Admitted to God, to ourselves and to another human being the exact nature of our wrongs.

6. Were entirely ready to have God remove all these defects of character.

7. Humbly asked God to remove our shortcomings.

8. Made a list of all persons we had harmed and became willing to make amends to them all.

9. Made direct amends to such people wherever possible, except when to do so would injure them or others.

10. Continued to take personal inventory and when we were wrong promptly admitted it.

11. Sought through prayer and meditation to improve our conscious contact with God, *as we understood Him*; praying only for knowledge of God's will for us and the power to carry that out.

12. Having had a spiritual awakening as a result of these steps, we tried to carry this message to others and to practice these principles in all our affairs.

The Twelve Steps of Divorce Recovery

---

1. We admitted we were powerless over others, that our lives had become unmanageable.

2. Came to believe that a Power greater than ourselves could restore us to wholeness.

3. Made a decision to turn our will and our lives over to the care of God, as we understood God.

4. Made a searching and fearless moral inventory of ourselves.

5. Admitted to God, to ourselves and to another human being the exact nature of our failings.

6. Were entirely ready to have God remove our defects of character.

7. Humbly asked God to remove our shortcomings.

8. Made a list of all persons we had harmed and became willing to make amends to them all.

9. Made direct amends to such people wherever possible, except when to do so would injure them or others.

10. Continued to take personal inventory, and when we were wrong, promptly admitted it.

11. Sought through prayer and meditation to improve our conscious contact with God, as we understood God; praying only for knowledge of His will for us and the power to carry that out.

12. Having had a spiritual awakening as a result of these Steps, we tried to carry this message to others and to practice these principles in all our affairs.

Chapter Three

The Twelve Steps
of Divorce Recovery

Step One

We admitted we were powerless
over others and that our lives had
become unmanageable.

Powerlessness is often a factor felt in divorce. During married life, a couple makes decisions together—for themselves, for their children, about their social life, their home and perhaps for elderly parents. After separation, we no longer have influence, or have much less influence, over our partner's decisions. We watch them go on without us to make decisions in new ways, and perhaps in ways we don't understand or approve of.

Dwelling on the decisions and behavior of others can send us into a tailspin because the imagination can create a nightmare that doesn't exist in reality, and even if it did, there would be little we could do about it. We can waste a lot of time thinking about our partner's actions. Obsessive thoughts whirl the mind like bald tires spinning on ice—using lots of energy but getting us nowhere and sometimes digging us in even deeper. This is one definition of "unmanageable."

Unfortunately, we are encouraged to think the worst of our partner during divorce. Attorneys operating in the adversarial mode exacerbate our negativity. Often the pervading philosophy is to *get* what we're entitled to, rather than to *share* what there is. In the attempt to protect their client, attorneys often do more damage than necessary by locking the couple into a conflict stance which slows things down while drastically increasing legal fees.

The antidote to this torture is to focus on our own responsibilities and actions. Applying the Twelve Steps to this process shows us a better way to proceed. How we apply the Steps in our lives depends on what our circumstances are at any given moment. Some of us are still living with a spouse, but we know the relationship is over. Only the physical move of people and possessions remains.

Some of us have just separated and are living on our own, perhaps for the first time in many years, experiencing the highs of freedom and the lows of loneliness, the thrill of making our own decisions and the pain of having no one to talk to.

Some of us are in the terribly uncomfortable legal process of divorce—being on the opposite side of the table from someone who once was our partner. Our children hang in the balance. Our home and personal possessions are in question. Nothing seems stable.

Some of us are in the numb healing stage—past the shock, through the legalities, and we need a quiet, low-stress environment in which to sort things out, to re-orient and even to re-create ourselves.

Some of us are beginning to reach out for new relationships—needing to test our newly found selves in social situations. We face the fear of another failure, of vulnerability, of more pain than we can stand. We may watch our former spouse begin to date others and possibly remarry.

The Twelve Steps apply and are helpful in all these stages. During this process it's so easy to obsess about and blame everyone else: our (ex)spouse, our children, friends who can't deal with the change, lawyers, etc. Although we must cope with all of them, it's important, for our own serenity, to realize that we can't *make* them do anything. We can, however, control our own behavior. We can be honest, open and caring. We can realize that, if we have children, we will likely be in touch with our ex-spouse until the children are independent—and even after that, at occasions like graduations, weddings and funerals. In other words, until one of us dies.

We are in charge of how we handle things and we'll live with these decisions for a long time. We can choose to end the marriage peacefully for the sake of the future times when our family will be together. We do this by monitoring our own behavior because the attitudes present during the divorce can prevail far into the future. Managing things well at the outset will save us much grief later. This, however, is the most difficult time to think ahead, but it's important to do the best we can.

> *Between stimulus and response,*
> *man has the freedom to choose.*
> —*Viktor Frankl*

Taking responsibility for our own behavior, regardless of the stimulus, means that our actions and reactions belong to us. We need to stop just reacting to others and make conscious decisions about what's helpful in the situation as a whole.

Often, when we choose our behavior wisely, our example influences others. At the least, our children will benefit. There should be at least one grounded person in the situation. We can decide to be that person.

Marianne Williamson has written this prayer to be used in the Ceremony of Divorce published in her book, *Illuminata*. It puts the past in a healthy perspective.

Dear God,
We ask You to take these two dearly beloved
        souls into Your hands.
Include in Your mercy and compassion their
        children.
May the golden cord that has bound these
        two in marriage be not violently severed,
        but carefully and peacefully laid aside, this
        act forgiven and granted meaning by God
        Himself.
May these two remain parents and sacred
        friends forever.
Never shall the bond of marriage be made
        meaningless, before God or humankind.
May these two beloved children of God remember
        that the love of their union was important,
        and honor it always.
Your experiences together were the lessons of lives
        lived searching for love.
God understands.
He asks you to remember the innocence in each other,
        now and forever.
May forgiveness wash you clean.

The love you gave and the love you received
        were real and will be with you always.
The rest, let us silently and willingly give to
        God, that He might heal your hearts and
        give rest to your souls.
You have suffered enough, in coming to this
        point.
With this prayer, may your family begin again,
        having released the past and sought from
        God Himself a new path forward.
We place both past and future in the hands
        of God.
May you remain so forever.
And so it is.
Amen.

These sentiments may seem almost perverse to those who are still feeling angry or bitter toward their spouse but they illustrate that a divorce doesn't eliminate all the positive elements that were present in the relationship and the marriage. Honoring this fact and acknowledging these feelings are actually helpful in recovery because they show us the positive and good in what we experienced.

Our son graduated from a very large university recently. Because there were 8,000 undergraduate seniors, plus masters and doctoral candidates graduating that day, only two tickets were allotted to each student—one for Mom and one for Dad. I was very glad that three years after the divorce his father and I could look each other in the eye without rancor and were able to take our son to lunch and enjoy it. It was Charlie's day and he wasn't torn apart or stressed out because his mom and dad were together for the day. We were still a family, but in a new context.

Choosing our actions wisely and foregoing judgment of others make our lives manageable.

Ideas for Working Step One

◆ Sort through what's causing you to feel stress today. Ask yourself if you are spending your energy trying to control the uncontrollable. If this is so, observe how you might be neglecting your own life in this attempt to accomplish the impossible.

◆ Think of ways to use this energy in your own life.

Step Two

Came to believe that a Power
greater than ourselves could
restore us to wholeness.

By "wholeness" we suggest that in any serious long-term relationship we invest a lot of ourselves in the other person. Whether or not the relationship was a good one, we sometimes feel that a piece of ourselves is missing when the relationship dissolves—the piece that was turned over to our partner when we merged as a couple. A simple illustration of this is that it doesn't take two people to pay the bills. One partner generally does it. When the couple breaks up and two households are created, the person who did not have that responsibility has to assume it again. This process of assuming responsibility spans the emotional, intellectual, physical, social and the financial areas.

Parenting responsibilities shift dramatically as well because the children's time will be divided between two households after a separation. One parent has total responsibility when the children are with him. Conversely, the other parent experiences being without the children. Both experience are new and can be overwhelming at first.

There are also those pieces of ourselves that were buried within to make us more compatible with our partner. For example, maybe we didn't tell jokes at a party because the attention embarrassed our partner; or perhaps we avoided making social arrangements with friends that our partner didn't like. Recovery from divorce includes reclaiming the parts of ourselves that were either unnecessary or put away to keep the peace as a couple. There is freedom and creativity in recovery work; possibilities for growth are everywhere.

Divorce is a major life transition, and change can be frightening as well as expanding. The process is made easier by having support. In divorce and separation our usual support network may weaken. Our spouse is gone, some of our friends are gone, our social structure has changed, our children are shaken and angry, our family may not understand.

A Twelve Step recovery group is one definition of a power greater than ourselves because it connects us to others who are going through, or have been through, the same traumatic experience. The bond formed in a group becomes a strong medicine—like taking an antibiotic for an infection. We'd probably heal anyway, but this speeds the process. It's very helpful to realize that we are not alone. There are others who may be further along and can give us some insight into what's to come and alert us to some of the pitfalls of divorce—such as using our children as bargaining tools or damaging the relationship with our spouse beyond civility.

IT TAKES TIME TO HEAL—ONE YEAR FOR EVERY FIVE YEARS OF MARRIAGE OR SERIOUS, LONG-TERM RELATIONSHIP. Don't rush it!

Another definition of a Power greater than ourselves, for those who believe—and this is not a prerequisite for the program—is God, the God of our understanding. This allows for a broad interpretation and expansion of our ideas as time goes on. No single religious definition is considered right or wrong. Defining God is left to the individual person. Whatever definition feels real is what counts.

The program teaches us that the Power greater than ourselves is benevolent and loving. Support for our individual process and acceptance of who and where we are is available to us in the steps and in a group.

Connection to others and eventually to our Higher Power are the beginning of our restoration to wholeness. We see proof that wholeness CAN be accomplished by the examples of those who have been in the program and have practiced the Steps.

I heard this interpretation of the words of Step Two at an Al-Anon meeting:

First I CAME to the meetings.

Then I CAME TO and realized that there were things to be learned. Maybe I didn't have *all* the answers yet.

Then I CAME TO BELIEVE, after hearing others speak, and began having some experiences of my own.

"Came to believe" is a key phrase because believing in, and relating to, a Higher Power is a slow process for most of us. Few of us begin with this belief in place.

When I began my Twelve Step process in Al-Anon, I felt that I was too sophisticated for the idea of a Higher Power. I thought that belief in a Higher Power was for people who were too weak to create their own reality. I knew what was best for me and I knew how to get it. "God helps those who help themselves—and only if they're lucky," I thought.

When the separation-divorce process began, however, I became overwhelmed with the many decisions that I had to make. Half of the time, I didn't have the answers. I had been a full-time mother of four children and had only a part-time job that didn't pay very well. Should I sell my house? Would it cause more damage to uproot the kids sooner, rather than later? Should I get a full-time job now or wait awhile so that I could be home more for them? Was the financial sacrifice worth it? What about the settlement—what should I ask for? How would the kids' college be paid for? Could I make enough money to take over when the settlement terms were over? There were many more questions than these, but you get the idea.

When decisions had to be made I remembered hearing people talk about how they asked for help and got answers. That prompted me to ask, too. I didn't really believe anything would change, but I had nothing to lose because I was unable to think clearly anyway. I felt totally alone and would have panic attacks when I woke up in the morning. They say that there's no such thing as an atheist in a foxhole. SOMEBODY OUT THERE—PLEASE HELP ME!

I began to realize that after I asked, and allowed for the possibility of an answer, something good happened. I met someone who would make a helpful suggestion. I found an article in the paper or a magazine that would have an answer for me. A good friend called or I was prompted to call someone. A check arrived in the mail just in time. I got the job I wanted. My son was accepted by his first-choice college, even though his grades weren't as good as they could have been.

I wouldn't always get exactly what I prayed for immediately, but I always got some guidance about the next step to take. I began to recognize this guidance and I now trust it and feel supported by it. After ten years of living like this, no one can convince me that a Higher Power doesn't exist.

Ideas for Working Step Two

♦   Keep an open mind.
♦   Allow the possibility of receiving love and help to come from a Power greater than yourself.

Step Three

Made a decision to turn our will
and our lives over to the care of
God, as we understood God.

When we practice the first two steps we begin to see that there is benevolence in our lives. Good things start to happen when we let go instead of attempting to control everything. Faith is built a step at a time with practice. The Twelve Steps are written in an order that encourages faith to grow. First, we admit that we are powerless in certain situations; then we come to believe that we can be restored, regardless of what others may or may not do; then, after seeing what can be accomplished by asking for guidance, we invite a Higher Power into our lives more and more often. No problem is too great or too small to ask about.

A minor example: at various times I've been delayed leaving my home or office and knew that I'd be late for an appointment. I felt tense and upset about it. I asked my Higher Power to get me there on time and then let go and relaxed. I ignored the clock on the dashboard. When I arrived, either I was on time, or the person with whom I had an appointment was also delayed, or it just didn't matter. In all of these instances no one was upset or inconvenienced. Most of the time I was the one kept waiting in the end.

A more significant example: I was worried about finding a high school for my son who was having academic difficulties in the public school. I asked my Higher Power for a solution and was led to a school that is designed for people who have undeveloped potential and that has had success in bringing out the best in this type of student. We already had looked at a number of schools, but when we found this one, both of us knew that it was the right place and he was accepted immediately.

Another example: I was told by people I trusted that to do my work I needed an advanced degree. Not having an undergraduate degree or a lot of extra time, I could not envision going through six years of school. I asked for guidance and found a college where I could complete a bachelor's degree in a short period of time because my college-level life experience was acceptable for credit. After asking for guidance I was led by various methods to the right answers within a few weeks.

Some of us already have faith in a Power greater than ourselves when we come into the program. Some of us have been turned off by religion in the past and haven't used prayer as a source of comfort and healing for a long time. Some of us have never had any religious training and have a hard time relating to the concept of God in the Twelve Steps. It doesn't matter where we are—only that we ask and remain open for answers. It can't hurt to experiment. Talk to God, ask for what you need and then be alert. You may see something on TV or in a magazine. A friend may call and say just the thing you need to hear. You may open to a page in a book, or see a picture in the newspaper that will give you an idea. Stay open to answers that are not exactly like the ones you envision; they may lead you to what you are asking for although not in the way you might expect.

After seeing evidence over a period of years that God moves in my life—and in better ways than I could think of myself—I have turned my will and life over to God's care. As I get out of bed I invite my Higher Power into my day. When I remember to do this, life is easier. There are no hassles, and people just seem to be more relaxed. Maybe it's them, or maybe it's my perception of them, but either way, I'm happier and life seems easier.

In contrast, when I try to force a situation or coerce someone into doing what I want or spend a lot of energy thinking about how I can control a situation so that it works in my best interests or the interests of a loved one, it doesn't produce the results I want. Sometimes, even if the situation does work out the way I want it to, the result isn't what I expected and can actually be disappointing. I end up regretting that I got involved.

It can take a lifetime to fully understand Step Three. Inherent in human nature, it seems, is the need to control, to thoroughly plan, to figure out in advance, to go through "what ifs?" When we integrate Step Three we realize that life is easier than we thought, we aren't as stressed and we don't feel so alone.

Divorce is a situation where the need to control is more pronounced than usual. Major changes occur. Our future is at stake. Our children and our financial security hang in the balance. It seems that life hinges on the divorce agreement.

What is not clear in the early stages and is often not addressed by the legal system—and what will *really* matter in the long run—is the relationship with our ex-spouse. No matter what papers are signed or what a judge may decide, it's the execution of the plans and the flexibility of the two parties that will make our future life peaceful or keep us tied up in tit-for-tat aggravation, denied access to the children and suffering financial instability.

Therefore, attention to the overall health of the situation will pay off in many ways later on. The relationship does not end with the signing of the papers unless there are no children and no spousal support in the agreement. In fact, if there are children, we will likely be connected to our spouse until one of us dies. There will always be some family business or celebration that both of us will want to be a part of. If both people maintain integrity, both people can share in an important event. If both parents can attend an event in peace, it's certainly easier on the child, and no one feels excluded.

How do we stay civil on these occasions? We take responsibility for our own behavior. We make a decision to stay sane, cooperative, unflappable and kind, whenever we can. This may sound like an impossible task, but it is possible more often than you might think and pays big dividends for us and for our children later on.

There are two thoughts to keep in mind at this time. First, if we behave with honesty and dignity, chances are that our partner will be more honest and dignified with us. If we hurl insults and show lack of trust, we are more likely to have that behavior returned. What goes around comes around.

Second, life goes on after the divorce. There will be many more opportunities. We'll meet new people and find new circumstances for fun and expansion. Divorce is not the end of the line. Divorce can actually be viewed as a gateway to a new life. Change can be good if we don't waste our lives fighting it. Our Higher Power (whether this means a support group, God, the Universe and so on) can help us expand our vision in this way. We can shift our perspective, at least part of the time, toward healthy growth and away from mourning and fear. Saying the Serenity Prayer can help us make that shift.

> *God, grant me the serenity*
> *to accept the things I cannot change,*
> *the courage to change the things I can*
> *and the wisdom to know the difference.*

In a Twelve Step group we use the phrase "turn it over." That means "God, you take care of it. I don't know what else to do." When we are out of options, *turn it over.* When we have tried everything we can think of, *turn it over.* When we are faced with a new problem, *turn it over.* When we are sure that we'll never get it all done, *turn it over.* We do our best. Then we let go and trust.

Our Higher Power is always working for our best interests, if we allow it. Our Higher Power enters by invitation. When we do this and then let go of control, remarkable solutions arise—better solutions than we probably would have thought of by ourselves. Let's be open to the wisdom that is available to us.

Ideas for Working Step Three

Take a coffee can, or any can with a plastic lid, and cut a slot in the plastic top. Cover the can with a piece of paper. It can be wrapping paper, plain white bond paper, or paper you've decorated. Write the words GOD CAN on it. Take a small piece of paper and write down what you are worried about or need help with. Fold the piece of paper up and drop it through the slot. Turn the can over and ask God to take care of the issue for you. Leave it there for awhile. This is a symbolic action of turning our will and our life to the care of God. What we can't, God can. I have done this exercise in my group, coming back to it the following week. We are always impressed by the number of people who receive some sort of answer.

Step Four

Made a searching and fearless
moral inventory of ourselves.

Although this sounds daunting, it's a wonderful opportunity for growth. Divorce, however, is like an emotional roller coaster, so pick a time when exploration feels like a good idea. Making this inventory in the context of the program we begin to see our strengths and shortcomings more clearly. This is essential to avoid repeating past mistakes. As we will explore later, *Recover or repeat* is one of our slogans.

The Steps never suggest beating ourselves up. No doubt we've done enough of that already, and it's not productive. What is productive is an honest look at ourselves—to take credit for what we see that we like and to work on what we don't like. Life goes on and we want to be ready.

With all the choices there are to be made, we can't know ourselves too well. The more we know, the better we can handle any situation. We'll understand what we need and why. We will know what we can give and what we can tolerate. We will recognize our shortcomings and begin to realize what we can do to strengthen ourselves.

When we avoid realizing our own responsibility in the demise of a relationship because of the possible pain involved, we also avoid taking hold of the power to change ourselves for the better. WE ARE IN CHARGE HERE.

We are not stuck forever in some irreparable pattern. *This is the place where we have enormous power—we can develop any attribute we choose.* When we understand what's missing, we can make the decision to develop what we need. It's what we *don't know* that hurts us. When we choose to stay blind to our shortcomings, we create the same scenarios over and over. Clarity helps us eliminate unsuccessful patterns.

We also recognize our strengths and understand that we can build on them in the future. It energizes us and gives us a lift to realize that, in spite of how we might feel today, we have done many things well and that we have tried hard to do our best. Our confidence and self-esteem are enhanced by this exploration because we see that while we've been human and capable of error, we also have many good qualities.

Progress, not perfection.

Practicing Step Four works very well when it's done in a group. It's good to know that others make the same mistakes we do, and sometimes we hear creative solutions that we can adopt for ourselves. This step helps us keep our humanity in perspective as well. We all make mistakes. We are no better or worse than someone else. Working Step Four helps us stay balanced—neither totally to blame nor totally innocent—in the situation and sets the stage for major growth.

The next few pages contains a list of characteristics that we either have or may want to develop. They are included for inspiration. Use them as affirmations. Read down the list and say them out loud. Take the ones that you like best and write them on a piece of paper with crayons or colored markers. Hang them where you will often see them. When we say or write I AM statements, like "I am learning to love myself," we absorb them into our behavior patterns.

I am...

...learning to love myself.
...learning to trust God.
...learning to trust other people.
...seeking help when necessary.
...asking for advice from positive people.
...telling the truth.
...speaking from the "I" point of view.
...saying what I mean but not saying it mean.
...being open to love others.
...able to draw boundaries.
...saying no when it's necessary.
...not pleasing others when it's harmful to myself.
...saying yes to life.
...forgiving others.
...understanding that my lack of forgiveness hurts *me* most of all.
...responsible for my serenity.
...responsible for my feelings and subsequent actions.
...following through; keeping my word.

...listening to others—without becoming defensive, thinking about what I'm going to say, or adding my own biography.

...apologizing when necessary.

...courageous but not abusive in the face of confrontation.

...able to diffuse, not exacerbate a difficult situation.

...able to put the children first.

...respecting the grieving process and being supportive of my children.

...refusing to put another person down when everyone else is doing it.

...doing a good day's work and feeling satisfied at the end.

...learning to smile often.

...having a kind word for others, even if I'm not feeling too great myself.

...patient, non-judgmental, happy and nice to be around.

...taving an interest in my appearance.

...seeking to be part of the solution, not part of the problem.

...avoiding talking just to hear myself talk.

...admitting when I don't know the answer.

...admitting that I was wrong, instead of making excuses for myself.

...seeking growth and maximizing my potential.

...realizing that I am capable, sincere, well-meaning, reliable, timely, creative and that I have many gifts, some developed and some yet to be discovered.

...taking one day at a time.

...learning to let go and let God.

...willing to practice turning things over to a Higher Power even when I doubt there is anyone listening.

On the next page you will find examples of searching and fearless moral inventory questions. Use them to explore your thinking. There are no right or wrong answers. Our own enlightenment is the goal of working Step Four.

A journal is a great tool for answering these questions. When we use a journal we have a tool for self-discovery and a documentation of our growth. Writing, whether in a notebook, a journal or on a computer becomes a way to reduce stress. When we awake at night, too angry to sleep—writing helps. When we are so angry we might explode, writing it out (maybe with red ink) helps discharge some of the excess energy.

In a group setting, these questions may be used as discussion topics giving each person a chance to answer. It's interesting to note that when we come back to these questions a few months later, our answers may be different. As with other types of inventory, some things increase in volume while others decrease, depending on the season. We grow and change all the time.

Step Four Questions

Moving On

A relationship has a filing system. When we fall in love, we only open the positive drawer. When we break up, we only open the negative one. The truth is that we are all composed of both drawers.

1. Am I willing to acknowledge that both sets of attributes exist in my partner?

2. And in myself?

3. Do I recognize the gifts that the marriage gave me?

4. Am I willing to admit and apologize for the mistakes I made in the marriage, or do I totally blame my partner?

5. Have I learned to take a break before making important decisions if I'm emotionally upset?

6. Have I learned to act instead of react?

7. Can I say what I mean and not say it mean?

8. Do I tell the truth?

9. Do I avoid exaggeration?

Taking Care of Myself

1. Am I taking care of myself well enough to preserve my own well being emotionally, mentally and physically?

2. Am I seeing a doctor, dentist or therapist, if necessary?

3. Am I choosing to be with supportive and positive people—friends who will support me rather than exacerbate my fears?

4. Am I exercising regularly to relieve stress?

5. Am I doing my best to be grateful for what is present in my life?

6. Am I cheerful in the company of others, or do I always take on the role of martyr?

7. Am I allowing myself to become overwhelmed with all there is to do, or am I slowing down to take one day at a time and to do what I can on that day?

8. Am I placing more value on material goods than on people?

9. Am I allowing myself to become too isolated, rather than calling a friend and making plans?

10. Am I looking for new friends whose lives are more like my own?

Dating Again

1. Is the main thing on my mind to connect with another man or woman as quickly as possible instead of working on myself and my recovery?

2. Do I expect someone to rescue me?

3. Am I waiting for Prince or Princess Charming to arrive?

4. Do I expect someone to complete me?

5. Am I waiting for someone to come along and "make it all better?"

6. Am I trying to be strong and independent before I begin to date?

7. Have I thought about the impact dating now will have on my children?

8. Do I realize that going out and having fun doesn't have to involve a romantic partner?

9. Do I believe that having another mate will solve all my problems?

Responsibility

1. Am I doing my best to minimize pain and suffering in my family?

2. Am I doing all I can to be sure everyone is well taken care of?

3. Am I acting in ways that create chaos or peace?

4. Have I fulfilled my personal potential?

5. Have I let someone else define me?

6. Even if it's not my idea to divorce and it's not my fault, am I doing the best I can to minimize damage—or out of pain and anger am I exacerbating damage?

Self-Absorption

1. Divorce is an emotional roller-coaster. Do I understand that although today might seem terrible, tomorrow may be different?

2. Am I aware that I am not the only one going through the loss?

3. Am I aware that the world goes on, regardless of how I feel today and that there are things that need to be done?

Child Issues

1. Do I realize that we are still a family—just redefined?

2. Do I realize that children are not responsible for their parents' decision to divorce?

3. Do I realize that my children have their own grief about the divorce?

4. Do I make things easier for them by not having them carry messages to the other parent?

5. Do I keep my promises to my children?

6. Am I mature enough to keep the children out of the middle of the marriage difficulties?

7. Am I reassuring the children that they are still loved by both parents?

8. Am I able to put the welfare of my children first without being vengeful or vindictive to their other parent?

9. Am doing the best I can to take care of my children financially?

10. Am I doing the best that I can to spend quality time with my children?

11. Am I leaning on my children too heavily for support instead of finding understanding adults who will listen without being directly affected?

12. Do I realize that the way I handle the divorce will effect the future of our family—that, having had children, we most likely will always be together at celebrations and on special occasions.

13. Do I consider their maturity level when giving information to my children?

Ideas for Working Step Four

Answer some of the questions on the preceding pages. Write them down in a notebook so you can refer to them again. It's interesting to notice how our perspective changes each time we answer the questions. After a few months have gone by, answer them again and note any changes or progress.

Step Five

Admitted to God, to ourselves
and to another human being the
exact nature of our failings.

Step Five helps us keep perspective. When we admit our failings to God we are forgiven. To admit them to ourselves is to take responsibility. When we admit our shortcomings to another human being we realize that we are human—no more, no less. Having someone listen to us and accept us helps us to heal. When going through divorce, it's important to have people to talk to. It helps if a few have undergone the divorce experience. This is another reason why a support group is helpful—it connects us with others, exposes us to their experiences, and we realize we aren't alone in making mistakes.

Practicing Step Five is the opposite of being in denial. Denial is useful when looking at the big picture is totally overwhelming, but we don't want to stay trapped there. When we admit to God, to ourselves and to someone else, we take a step out of denial. While our shortcomings float around undefined inside us, we don't have to do much about them, but when we openly admit them, even if it's just to ourselves, we can never be totally blind to them again. Believe it or not, this is good.

When we bottle up our guilt, fear, sadness and frustration, they seem to grow like mold in an old bag of bread. Allowing sunshine and air to flow in by talking things over with someone else diminishes the negative build-up.

Catholics will tell you that when they leave the confessional, they feel better. They have talked their shortcoming over with someone else and feel forgiven by God and man. Even though entering confession can be challenging, when it's over a feeling of relief often follows. Practicing Step Five doesn't add to our guilt, it lessens it.

As a general rule, it's best to be with supportive people during this major transition. People who are negative, critical or uninterested can undermine our progress. Who needs that? Remember that the main goal of the Steps is to heal ourselves, not to beat ourselves up. People who are going through the same situation, but perhaps are further along, are often beneficial to be around. Verbalizing our thoughts brings a feeling of release. It makes us feel better to let stored-up things out constructively, instead of blowing up inappropriately at someone or over something that happens to get in our way.

I've noticed that the more guilt I feel, the nastier I am. I'm short-tempered, feel ill-at-ease and try to rationalize my actions or punish myself about the deed or lack of action. If, instead, I talk about it with someone I trust, I release some of the pent-up feelings and I'm able to act in a kinder, gentler fashion—both to myself and to the people around me. This was especially true when I was at home with young children. If I yelled at them too often, I felt bad. The worse I felt, the more I yelled. The more I shouted, the worse I felt. You get the picture. Facing and admitting our shortcomings help us *stop the behavior*. The more conscious we become about a mistake, the sooner we can banish it from our system of behavior.

We work Step Five to avoid making the same mistakes over and over again. If we recognize that an aspect of our behavior is standing in the way of getting what we want or need, then we can act differently and get different results.

Uncovering our failings and making them more real by admitting them—first to God, then to ourselves and then to another human being—gives us more control over our own behavior. This is what appealed to me most about this step. I wasn't interested in being perfect as much as I was in being in control of myself. I wanted to make decisions about my own behavior and be able to stick with them. I wanted to feel that I could stay calm in an upsetting situation, that I wouldn't overreact to negative statements, that I wouldn't lose my temper with my children and that I could generally stay sane and act appropriately. Let's face it—divorce tests our normal limits in many ways. We may have to change our living arrangements, see less of our children, get another job, have less money, have to appear in court and argue our side of the story, or eventually begin a new relationship. We would benefit from being clear on what we have done and have left undone in the past so that we can begin our new life with a fresh perspective. Talking things out with a person we trust helps us to stay honest and keep our perspective as we listen and respond to them and they to us.

I have found the practice of this Step to be extremely rewarding, particularly in regard to my children. I have made mistakes as a parent. I haven't been perfect, and while I've tried hard to do a good job, I've fallen short by becoming impatient, sometimes critical and by leaning on my older children too much during the divorce. Practice of Step Five has helped us discuss these issues openly. Communication lines are open and are kept open when we apologize for our shortcomings.

I have also done this with my ex-husband. After some time apart, I could see more clearly how I contributed to the demise of our marriage and have apologized for it. Apology keeps the resentment level down. This is important because we have to deal with each other in regard to our children. It felt good to clear the air and even if he couldn't do the same, *I* felt better and that's what counts.

Ideas for Working Step Five

Call a friend you trust. Make arrangements to get together where you can speak privately. Explain to him what you are about to do in sharing your issues. His job is to listen. Your job is to put your issues on the table. As you discuss these issues, you will see them more clearly. Perspective is the goal of Step Five and talking to a supportive friend will help us attain it.

Step Six

Were entirely ready to have God
remove our defects of character.

To practice Step Six we recognize our shortcomings and ask ourselves if we want to give them up. The obvious answer is *yes*, but some of our defects are considered by us to be, in some ways, an integral part of our personality.

For example, I drive too fast. Should I slow down? Of course—it's dangerous to myself and others. Do I? Maybe. Part of me thinks it's cool to zip in and out of lanes and pass people. Driving too fast is also connected to my inability to budget my time—because I allow less than I should. Am I *really* willing to change all of that?

Smoking is another good example. We know that smoking isn't good for us, and it's not good for those around us. How many smokers try again and again to quit and are unsuccessful until someone or something really motivates them? Smoking, in the mind of a smoker, has positive qualities as well as the obvious negatives.

Denial is also a factor, because before we're ready to give up our defects, we tell ourselves that they aren't *that* bad. We rationalize and are defensive about them. We think of reasons to perpetuate the negative behavior. We believe we *have to* or that we *really like* doing these things—they are important to us. To become willing to let go of our defects is often much more involved than it seems.

Defects of character are behaviors or beliefs that stand in the way of getting what we need or want. For example, two things I've always loved—singing and sports—became increasingly difficult for me after smoking cigarettes for many years. My children were upset about my smoking because they were taught in school that it's dangerous. Second-hand smoke affected their lungs also. My inability to stop smoking was a defect of character that I needed to admit and work to change. Eventually I gave up smoking, my kids were relieved, and I was quickly able to sing and do the physical activity I enjoyed. Giving it up was difficult, but I learned to focus on all the things I could make better if I stopped smoking rather than on how much I was suffering from the loss of cigarettes.

It's helpful to make a list of what we consider to be our shortcomings in one column and then in another column write the opposite or positive trait, or one that we want to develop in its place. It's easier to replace a behavior than give one up. We need to *do something positive,* not merely give up the negative. Don't deny yourself—do something different! Practice the positive behavior.

Defects	Replace With
Driving too fast	Driving carefully
Impatience	Patience
Being judgmental	Being accepting
Impulsiveness	Being rational
Co-dependence	Independence
Lashing out verbally	Being kind
Self-centeredness	Consideration of others
Aggressiveness	Gentleness

| Bullying | Compassion |
| Arrogance | Humility |

During separation and divorce it's in our best interest to take responsibility for our half of the problems in the relationship. Even if we see ourselves as the victim and our partner as flagrantly out of line, there were still two people in the union. If we were victims, why did we choose and then stay with a partner who hurt us? Were we blind? Were we in denial? Do we want to do that again? Do we want to repeat the pattern in other areas? If anything good can come of this painful process, let it be that we learn from our mistakes. Let us grow and expand and attract a different type of experience as we go forward.

Practicing Step Six while going through a divorce improves the end result of that divorce in many ways. There is so much fear to deal with because the familiar is suddenly replaced by the unfamiliar. Fear of the unknown and intense emotional pain can amplify our negative personality traits. We are more likely to snap, jump to conclusions and attack during divorce. Some of us want more than our share of the marital property; some of us choose not to support our children appropriately; some lie under pressure; others become vengeful; some of us whine and complain; some of us won't help ourselves take the next step. We may take out our negative state of mind on our children, who are the innocent victims of this process. We may be punitive to our (ex)spouse by using our children as a weapon, which is *never* a good idea.

Some of these defects are present in most people going through divorce. It takes strength and courage to rise above the trenches of the divorce battle and see the big picture. That's where the Twelve Step practice is so helpful. We don't have to do this alone. If we ask, our Higher Power will help us become more objective and provide us with the guidance and inspiration to get through this painful time with grace and dignity.

Awareness of our defects is helpful, and when we become willing to let go of them, we will be spared regret at the end of the divorce. We're not expected to be without flaws in this step—only to increase our self-knowledge and wisdom so that we can move forward in a positive, creative and intact way.

> *Here is a test to find whether your mission*
> *on earth is finished: if you're alive, it isn't.*
> —Richard Bach, *Illusions*

There is a difference between realizing our shortcomings and actually wanting to let go of them. Becoming ready to let go of behaviors that are standing in our way to wholeness is the focus of Step Six.

The goal of this program is to improve ourselves in an atmosphere of non-judgmental support so that we don't make the same mistakes again.

Ideas for Working Step Six

Make the decision to drop self-defeating behaviors. Write a list of shortcoming you want to eliminate and decide which one to eliminate first. As you eliminate one, choose another to work on. This process is a lifelong endeavor.

Step Seven

Humbly asked God to remove
our shortcomings.

It's not uncommon after doing Steps Four and Five to see things we don't like about ourselves. The process often goes something like this:

Step 4. To recognize
Step 5. To admit
Step 6. To want to change
Step 7. To realize that we
        need support in making those changes.

Change is difficult. Letting go of long-ingrained, habituated behavior takes focus and determination. With our Higher Power's help, our own determination, and the support of a group and perhaps of a therapist, great and permanent changes are possible. *Ask and we shall receive* has been the experience of most of us who have been in the program for a while. Almost all of us have had at least one experience of asking for strength, courage, serenity or assistance to cope with a situation and having it arrive. From this initial reaching out, faith grows. If we aren't ready to give up our shortcomings, they can't be removed. It's our choice.

Humility is an underrated characteristic and a key ingredient in this step. Some of us think that being humble means putting ourselves down or subjecting ourselves to abuse by others, but humility is defined in Webster's Dictionary as *having or showing a consciousness of one's defects or shortcomings.* Humility doesn't mean that we should exaggerate them or feel terrible about them—just be aware of these shortcomings.

Humility can also mean that we're no better or worse than anyone else, that we're not perfect and we don't have to know all the answers. It means that we don't have to take care of everyone else—that it may not even be appropriate to do so. We don't have to lecture others about how to behave. This is very good news because the up-side of humility is that we only have to take care of our own business. If we stop thinking about other people's behavior, we'll have more time to develop ourselves.

Cultivating humility allows us to learn and therefore to continue to grow. If we believe we know everything already, we are closed to new information. Buddhist teachings refer to the "beginner's mind" where we are encouraged to look at life from a new perspective. As an example, pick up an orange as if you've never seen one before: study it...smell it...feel the shape... peel it...taste it. Take your time and focus on the sensations. Really enjoy it. You can do this with something as small as a single raisin. Taking this attitude gives a fresh perspective on the most normal, everyday experiences. I encourage you to try this experiment. You will see the orange in a new way. It's an interesting and powerful experience.

Thinking with the beginner's mind injects freshness and enthusiasm into our relationships and into our daily routine, enabling us to become more conscious of life's opportunities to love and its many simple pleasures.

Human beings are very complex. A deadly threat to any relationship is to assume we already know all there is to know about a person. We can't possible know everything because we change and grow all the time. Relationships become stale by thinking a person does not change year to year.

We can practice the beginner's mind in our relationships by looking at people differently. Try looking at a person you know well (child, parent, co-worker, friend) as if he or she is a stranger. Without judgment, observe the whole picture—the posture, mode of dress, texture of the hair, the expression around the eyes and the mouth. Is the person happy, excited, tense, absorbed, depressed, looking well? Observe the hands. Are they relaxed or clenched? How about the shoulders—up around the ears, or lower and relaxed?

What is this person doing? Why? What has she experienced today? Has she met new people? Read something interesting? Learned something new? Changed her mind? Ask a question. Start a conversation. Explore! Most important of all, listen carefully to the answer with your ears, eyes, heart and mind.

In Step Seven we recognize our shortcomings and humbly admit that we are unable to give them up totally by ourselves. Most of us need support to stay alert and not fall backward into old patterns—so, we ask our Higher Power for the strength to change. If you have trouble with the idea of God or a Higher Power, you can get support from a Twelve Step Group or from a trusted friend, but other people can't take away our defects.

For people who haven't tried this, I know it's hard to believe. Many of us think that the changes can only be made by sheer will or determination. I can tell you that I have tried forcing myself to change and it hasn't always worked. Old habits are hard to break. Once we understand why we want to make the change, asking for help really makes it easier and possible.

Experiment with the concept of a Higher Power; it isn't necessary to absolutely believe in God to get the benefits. Just be open to the possibilities. Concede that while you're not sure, you're willing to be open to the idea. You've got nothing to lose by trying this or, as we say in the Twelve Step movement, *act as if... .*

> *Assume a virtue if you have it not.*
> —*William Shakespeare*

To *act as if* means to try on a behavior that you wish to develop. For example, you're invited to a party where you won't know most of the people. You're nervous and would like to feel more confident. Rather than focusing on how uncomfortable you are, act as if you're totally at home in this situation. What would you do then? Would you smile more, begin more conversations, have a more open attitude? If you act as if you're having a good time you'll be more relaxed than if you focus on your discomfort. With practice you'll see that you actually will be more comfortable.

So in the spiritual realm, in acting as if you do believe in God and that your prayers will be answered, what would you want to happen? Suspend disbelief for a moment and have an open dialogue with this Presence. Ask for what you need and then try to keep an open mind. You may or may not get an answer immediately, but you *will* get one. You may not get exactly what you ask for, but you will be led in the right direction. Insights come from unexpected sources. People who are new at this call it coincidence. Those of us who have experience know better.

When you look back, a few months down the line, you will notice new positive qualities have replaced the defects. We can all benefit by recognizing our shortcomings, admitting them, being willing to change and asking God to help us by taking away our self-defeating tendencies.

Ideas for Working Step Seven

Take the list you made in Step Six and put it in the God Can. Be sure you actually ask your Higher Power to remove the shortcomings as you do this.

Step Eight

Made a list of all persons we had
harmed and became willing to make
amends to them all.

Until now all the work has been internal and self-focused. Step Eight asks us to look deeply into our relationships with other people and learn from them. No one is perfect; we all have work to do. We are asked to examine ourselves in relationship to others, to learn from them and to become willing to change.

To make a list of persons we have harmed and to become willing to make amends is the first step in awareness of how our behavior has affected others. It's much easier to stay focused on our own point of view and rationalize our own behavior than to look openly and honestly at our mistakes and become willing to make amends.

Sometimes we have to put ourselves at the top of the list. In the divorce process, with all the many things we need to think about, we may neglect ourselves. Maybe that was true during the marriage as well. Maybe we didn't stand up for ourselves enough; maybe we served others to the point of our own deterioration. Maybe we didn't see doctors and dentists when we should have, or maybe we allowed ourselves to become exhausted by overwork. As mentioned before, divorce can be a gateway to new, healthier behavior and that is why we take this step.

When the list has been written and we become willing to make amends to those we harmed, we feel a release from guilt. Guilt is a good teacher when it points us in the right direction, but it can be poisonous when left to fester. Working Step Eight reduces paralyzing guilt. Feeling really bad about ourselves is like swimming in mud. We can easily get confused and defensive. Doing Step Eight work clarifies for us what our 50 percent is. Consciousness is the goal of the Twelve Step process. By physically writing down a list, we make it real and see clearly where our mistakes have been made. Marriage, in the author Madeleine L'Engle's words, is "a two-part invention." The failure of a marriage is rarely 100 percent one-sided. If we see our own shortcomings and forgive them, it helps us to forgive others.

It seems that we go through periods of thinking *it's all my fault* and then switch to *it's all their fault*, and we toggle back and forth between the two. Eventually, and sometimes this takes years, we come to a balanced perspective. Step Eight speeds awareness along because working it helps us clarify our own role in this painful situation. We are not meant to take more responsibility than our own—just our own, whatever that may be—not to punish ourselves, but to move on. This understanding will put us in the driver's seat because we will recognize our mistakes or misjudgments and we can choose not to repeat them. We can choose to be attracted to a different type of person. We can choose not to fall into the same behavior patterns. We can choose to take our time, heal and learn new ways from people who are good examples.

If we take a high-and-mighty stance, thinking that we are totally innocent of creating our current situation, we won't learn anything. We'll find it hard to forgive and consequently to find peace for ourselves.

Because of the considerable pain experienced in divorce, we may become self-absorbed—losing perspective on how what we do and say (and what we don't do and say) affects other people. Aside from ourselves, our children are the people who suffer the most. They don't have any power to change the situation. We make the decisions that drastically affect their lives, and they have to accept it; so in some ways, they have it harder than we do.

We may forget that the relationship with our spouse will go on for as long as we are parents, and we may strike at him or her out of fear and anger. We may react out of defensiveness and not think a situation through. Our parents and parents-in-law may suffer if they love the partner of their son or daughter. They worry about the family as a whole, and fear of losing their son- or daughter-in-law and contact with their grandchildren. We may reject friends of our spouse without thinking about how they may feel.

All of these situations are common in divorce and we will surely fall into some of these traps, but we don't have to stay there. We can face what we've done squarely and honestly by making a list. There's something about writing things down that makes them more concrete. We look at that list, and as we do, we decide to become willing to make amends and restore the relationships and foster forgiveness. Even if we can't change things immediately, we can become aware and avoid piling up even more guilt for the future. We feel lighter and have more hope for the future after doing this. We can decide to become proactive rather than reactive.

Unaware of our shortcomings, we remain in a repetitious cycle without knowing why. Aware of them, we become willing to let them go, ready to ask God for support in making the necessary changes and willing to think about others in our lives. We can clear up the guilt we have accumulated in the past. We can apologize for our part. We can make decisions to be a better parent, friend, family member and co-worker.

We are on our way out of self-defeating patterns. Life, with self-awareness, can be liberating and a lot more stable. We begin to understand that we have the untapped power to change ourselves. We can be who we *choose* to be.

Ideas for Working Step Eight

Once you have made a list of the people you have harmed, think about what you can do to remedy the situation. Are you willing to remedy the situation?

Step Nine

Made direct amends to such people
whenever possible, except when to do
so would injure them or others.

Step Nine is the first step where we practice what we have learned and "step" outside of our own mental, emotional and spiritual arena. As discussed in Step Eight, we may owe amends, apologies or changes in behavior to our (ex)spouse, our children, our parents or parents-in-law, friends and also to ourselves. Facing our misdeeds and taking responsibility for them—by apologizing, returning what we've borrowed, becoming more patient, telling the truth and so forth—restores us to a natural and more positive mental framework. We no longer have to follow unconscious programming. Practicing the Twelve Steps places the power of action in the HERE AND NOW. When we look to ourselves for action, we realize that there's no situation too difficult to be bettered in some way.

We can say that we are truly sorry or ask, if appropriate, if there's anything we can do to make amends. This does not necessarily mean that the decision to divorce is a mistake or that we should live with a destructive situation; it means that we can apologize for *our* part in the situation. It's important to think about whether our actions or words might cause harm rather than help. If there is any hurt involved, we may not be making amends, we may be seeking revenge. Revenge does not bring us peace. It creates or continues a vicious cycle. Maybe we only need to say a prayer for someone and keep our distance.

During separation and divorce, it becomes critical to communicate clearly, to avoid jumping to conclusions and to clarify often. When we're in pain, it's easy to become defensive and perceive an attack when, perhaps, none was intended. The entire family is on edge, everyone feels threatened, and this is entirely understandable. Change is on the horizon. Whether you were the person who made the decision to divorce, their partner, or a peripheral family member, some fear is inevitable. Few of us welcome this kind of change, and everyone is uncomfortable with loss. It's easy, under these circumstances, to panic, to try to grab as much as we can and to snap at people. Kindness, consideration, generosity, humility, honesty and peace are qualities that are hard to come by. Even those who normally have a high degree of these qualities are sorely tested during divorce.

When we were dealing with the separation agreement I felt inept because I had no experience with legal agreements or with most financial matters. My husband, in contrast, was a professional negotiator, a public accountant and had paid the bills throughout our 23 years of marriage. I found myself in a panic every time I had to discuss these subjects. Emotions ran high and I was scared. I knew it would be easy to lose control. My husband was very comfortable with financial matters, but very uncomfortable with issues concerning our four children. I knew how to deal with issues concerning them. He felt inept on that level, so he was vulnerable too. My attorney advised me not to get emotional during these negotiations—good advice, but how was I going to do that? How was I going to avoid becoming defensive, using the kids to manipulate the negotiations, and risk escalating an already volatile situation? We had been on the same side for 23 years, and now we were opposing each other.

I wanted to do things differently than I had before. I wanted to shore myself up and act like an adult instead of a frightened child. I knew I'd have more self-control if I felt comfortable, so I created a setting that would maximize my feelings of security and serenity. We were already separated so I told my husband that negotiations would be easier for me on the phone. This gave me a sense of safety, because I could always hang up if things got nasty. Next, I looked over the paperwork in advance so the details would be fresh in my mind. Then I played relaxation music softly in the background and burned incense during the phone conversations. I created my own personal environment that made me feel safe and no one else had to know about it. All of this kept me from losing it emotionally, kept things moving forward in a positive way and I was able to avoid reactions that could have made our divorce a lot worse. If I stayed calm, he stayed calm. Although I was taking care of myself, I was also aware of the difficulties we had had in the past when I got upset and wanted to flee from financial discussions. I wanted to reduce fear, feel competent and avoid having to make even more amends in the future.

It takes only one person doing things differently to change a situation. When one person breaks old patterns, the other almost has to because most relationship problems take two people to keep them going. Imagine a boxing match with only one fighter. He can dance around for a while, but it's not as interesting as having someone to fight with. The game, as we knew it, can't be played because the rules have changed. When one person changes, there's a ripple effect around him or her. Positive attitudes and statements are stronger and more attractive than negative ones, and the positive aspects will increase if just one person chooses to alter the pattern. So, if you're going into a situation that you know will be difficult, prepare in advance. Think about what would help you be more comfortable and feel safe, and do your best to be proactive in those ways. It really makes a difference.

Some of the angst in divorce is created by the couple indulging in vengeful power plays and hurling mean-spirited remarks at each other. Becoming embroiled in these scenarios takes the relationship from bad to worse. Lawyers back up their clients, so there are four people fighting, which makes for double trouble. Competitiveness, nastiness, greed and revenge are considered normal in this situation and are expected by the system, but it doesn't *have* to be that way. Marriage, unlike the legal process, is an emotional enterprise a well as a practical one. Divorce evokes a clash of those two levels. It's impossible to distill years of marriage into a black and white legal document and have it become the ultimate vehicle for working everything through. Typical legal solutions are insufficient in this process because the law is intellectual and people are emotional. Much of what happens is subject to interpretation. The interpretation is based on how people felt in the past as well as how they feel in the present, and feelings change from day to day and even from moment to moment.

Stay conscious of what's going on. Don't assume that anyone else knows better than you do about how to handle the end of your marriage. Don't turn all power over to attorneys, thinking that they know best about everything. They work best when we do our homework, get involved in decision making, and stay as calm and as peaceful as possible. All it takes is one person who refuses to be caught up in negative, self-defeating actions to pre-empt what could be an emotional and financial disaster. One person can create momentum toward a more peaceful parting, with assets shared and children spared the emotional damage that goes with seeing their parents tear each other apart.

Regardless of how we have lived up until today, we can make decisions to live differently now and have less to make amends for in the future. The present—today—is what counts.

Ideas for Working Step Nine

A simple apology is often enough to accomplish Step Nine, and people appreciate the effort. Be sure your motivation is pure before you proceed. It's important not to have any expectations from the other person. This is a one-way exercise—from you to them. Clearing the air, alleviating guilt and creating peace for yourself are its goals.

Step Ten

Continued to take personal inventory,
and when we were wrong promptly
admitted it.

Here is a good question from *A Course In Miracles:*
"Would you rather be right or be happy?" It takes so much
energy to remain in a "right" stance and justify our behavior, never looking at other possibilities. Step Ten asks us to
realize and accept that we aren't perfect; we are
human—no more, no less. Major changes in behavior
don't usually happen overnight; it's easy to slip back
temporarily. We do, however, need to acknowledge
mistakes, to choose again to make amends and to do the
right thing. Because the decision to divorce and the subsequent changes that divorce precipitates are so difficult, we
may cope in a way that's sometimes less than our best.

Apology, like humility, is vastly underrated. Some
think that to apologize is to admit weakness, but the
opposite is actually true. Everyone makes mistakes and
most of us make a lot of them. A person who can admit a
mistake can be trusted and respected. Rationalizing and
justifying an error confuses and exasperates others and
takes much more time and effort than a simple apology
that demonstrates honesty and integrity. When an apology
is made, the issue has closure. The deed doesn't stay on
your mind: *I should have done this, I shouldn't have said that; I
should have been more careful or considerate.* Instead we may
think: *I made a mistake. I wish I hadn't done that, but I did. I'm*

sorry. I will learn from my mistake and make a sincere attempt to stop this behavior. This lightens the load immediately. Mistakes are a part of life. If we don't make them, we aren't living. When we spend energy hiding our mistakes, or denying them, we create bigger problems than existed in the first place.

It always works to our advantage in the long run to admit a mistake, to apologize and move on. With practice, this becomes a habit, and soon we can't tolerate those negative guilt feelings building up internally. We choose to deal with them as soon as possible—for our own sake and for the sake of others.

Admitting we were wrong sets a good example for our children. They learn from us that it's human to make mistakes, that we can forgive ourselves and ask for forgiveness from others. Apology enhances our relationships with our children. Too often we hold back an apology because we think it turns power over to them and they will hold the admission of error over us, when, in reality, an apology allows us to get out of our *right* stance and open up some real dialogue. Our willingness to admit faults allows them to do the same. Honest communication clears the air and makes everyone feel better. This is especially true during the upheaval of divorce.

Taking responsibility for our own behavior and realizing and admitting our mistakes as soon as we can enables us to work through problems with others. In doing this, we avoid adding more guilt to the pile.

When guilt builds, it makes everything worse. We may become defensive, self-destructive and closed off. It's healthier and smarter to take care of this right away. Life becomes a lot cleaner and clearer.

When I began a new job and had to learn new business procedures I was grateful to have already realized that mistakes are normal. No one likes to make them, but they are a part of life. When I make a mistake, I apologize, make a sincere attempt to correct it and move on. I don't beat myself up and I don't let anyone else do it to me either.

Ideas for Working Step Ten

Admit, own up and accept your own mistakes. Don't agonize, justify, rationalize or feel threatened by them. You are a human being. Mistakes come with the territory. Apologize, rectify the situation if necessary, and move on.

Step Eleven

> Sought through prayer and meditation
> to improve our conscious contact with
> God, as we understood God, praying only
> for knowledge of His will for us and the
> power to carry that out.

I can imagine those of you who have a problem with the idea of God, or a Higher Power, saying "Yeah, sure. Do I have to be Mother Theresa? I'm not like that—I can't pray only for what *God* wants! God helps those who help themselves, right? I know what I want. If I pray at all, I'll ask for what *I* want." There's a reason that this step is number Eleven, rather than Step One or Two. Please don't be impatient with yourself or give up too soon. Twelve Step work is a self-improvement journey with no time limitations.

We all interpret the Steps in our own way and that's fine. There is no right or wrong way to practice them. However, it's good to be willing to expand the mind. Some of us have had a difficult time with religion in the past. Keep in mind that religion is not God. God is bigger than any religion. Religion provides a path to God, but only that. Please don't let a problem from the past or lack of early training block your willingness to be in contact with the Higher Power. You will only short-change yourself.

The Steps have been in existence for 60 years, and thousands of people use them daily in many ways. I was skeptical, too, when I began working with them ten years ago. Yet, so many people before me were able to make major life changes—it seemed possible that even if I didn't understand the Steps at first, they were probably still worth pursuing. I didn't want to ignore anything that would help me move on from where I was. After living through a divorce, I was willing to look at any tool if it would take away the pain and help me grow. I had an opportunity to change things, and I wanted to do it the best way I could.

For thousands of years great spiritual minds have tried to explain the existence of God and the many paths leading us to our Higher Power. I'm not a theologian nor a philosopher. I can only share my own spiritual process and what I have learned from others during the past five years while leading a Twelve Step Divorce Recovery Group. I can guarantee, however, that working the Steps will improve your life.

For me, maintaining conscious contact with God is simple now. After years of searching for "right" answers I have found that when I ask, I get help. It may not be exactly what I've asked for, but it will get me where I want to go faster and better than I could have on my own. When I get up in the morning, I ask God to be with me during that day. The energy around me must change because people respond to me differently. People are nicer and the day goes better than when I forget to issue the invitation.

Joseph Campbell, a wonderful teacher, philosopher and writer suggested that we "follow our bliss." I believe that when we follow what makes us deeply happy, pursue what we are passionate about and do what we know represents our true self—we are doing what is "God's will for us." That's how we know that we're on the right track. We recognize it by the joy it brings.

All of us are on the earth for a reason. We all have our unique piece in the All-that-is. I believe that humanity is like a giant jigsaw puzzle, and the whole picture isn't complete until our piece is added. When everyone is in touch with his or her true gift, the puzzle will be complete. Every single piece is important and has the same value as every other piece. My concept is that God is the Energy under the puzzle like a table, a support, a foundation, a place where we can rest, an energy that is under us all the time. We may not be conscious of it, but it's there just the same. Can you imagine doing a jigsaw puzzle without using something to support the pieces while you work on it?

To me, "praying only for knowledge of His will for us" means we ask what we must do to take our place in the big picture so that we can feel that joy and peace. We don't have to be missionaries or give up all worldly possessions and so forth (unless, of course, that *is* our particular bliss). We just need to find our place. When we do, we'll see that people support us, materials present themselves, doors swing open and the traffic clears up. This is what having "the power to carry that out" means. Things seem to flow easily in our direction because God wants us to be happy and to do the work that is most satisfying for us. We do our best work when we love it. This is our birthright!

We need to ask for the information in prayer and to listen for answers in meditation. Meditation is a practice used to slow the mind and body down so that we can hear new information. It isn't difficult; it only requires practice. A racing mind won't be open to the information that comes. Inspiration may have been trying to get through to us for years, but dedicated to our hustle-bustle lives, we emit a busy signal. Sometimes circumstances slow us down so we can pay attention. Maybe this is why we get sick. The common cold could be a message to slow down, take care of ourselves and pay attention—there's a message trying to get through. Believe me, meditation is a lot more pleasant than getting sick.

There are different styles of meditation and many books have been written on the subject. There are audio tapes available that can assist you in reaching a relaxed state of mind. There are guided meditations that include a person's voice taking you into and out of visualizations, tapes of musical instruments only and those with soothing sounds like the ocean, the rain or sounds from the forest. I play tapes on a walkman for maximum impact during meditation and use the music tapes on the stereo when someone is tense, sick or can't sleep. It really makes a difference in the atmosphere as they are played. Do this for yourself.

Whether or not we change our direction after we get the message is up to us. I believe we are all here to heal each other, to teach each other and to enhance each other's lives. If we were doing this for one another, heaven would be here right now. I think the end of the world as we know it will come when all the puzzle pieces are in place and then we'll all move on to a higher dimension together. While there's even one piece missing, we can't go—that's how important we all are.

Step Eleven shows us the way to connect. When we practice this step we feel safe; we know we are supported; we feel connected to others and where we should be. We know that we are not alone.

Ideas for Working Step Eleven

Ask your Higher Power for guidance on whatever situation you need help with. Hold the problem in your mind for a moment and then visualize it floating away like a helium balloon.

If you are new to meditation, here's one example of how to do it. There are many different forms. Have your pen and journal handy.

1. Put some soothing, gentle, non-distracting music on. The radio won't work for this because of commercial interruptions.

2. Sit up straight in a comfortable chair with your feet on the floor, arms and legs uncrossed and hands open on your lap. Close your eyes and begin to breathe slowly and deeply. Inhale for a count of six and exhale for a count of eight.

3. Wherever you find you're holding tension in your body, unclench the muscles. Just breathe and try to keep your mind as free as possible. If a troubling thought comes through, just let it float by. Mentally ride the music.

4. Stay with it for about twenty minutes. When tempted to get up, tell yourself that this is your time and you deserve this gift.

5. Come out of the meditation by slowly moving your hands, massage your face and stretch a bit. Meditation may end here. You will get thoughts during the day that pertain to your question, so be alert to them as they present themselves. They might come while in the shower, when you're driving or doing some automatic task, like washing dishes.

6. OR you can pick up your journal and pen and start writing. JUST START WRITING. Write the first thing that comes into your mind. Don't judge it, re-read it or analyze it while you are writing. Don't stop for spelling, punctuation or any kind of nit picking. Put the journal down when you are finished and read it later. You may find what you wrote very interesting.

A relaxation tape is worth the investment. You can find them in the New Age section of most music stores. If you can't find them, ask a sales person.

Step Twelve

> Having had a spiritual awakening as a
> result of these steps, we tried to carry
> this message to others and practice
> these principles in all our affairs.

The gift of a spiritual awakening is amazing. We realize that no matter what the circumstance, we are not alone and without resource. We learn that we can change, grow and choose the way we lead our lives. We learn about our Higher Power's love for us and that good things are coming. Grace comes with or without our awakenings but it comes faster and more often when we invite and allow the God-Energy into our lives.

When we give up managing everything and everyone, take responsibility for what is truly ours, turn over the rest to God, and become aware of our own behavior toward others and ourselves, we begin to experience serenity.

Serenity is the basis for a sane life. True peace comes from being connected with our inner selves and our Higher Power, not by blaming others and holding grudges. Peace is the commodity we all need the most, although that's often not understood or acknowledged during divorce. When our minds and bodies are quiet, we can make better and more compassionate decisions. We become *pro*active out of thought, choice and decision rather than *re*active to pressure, events and the behavior of others. We are better parents, we can do our jobs, we can laugh more easily, we are more creative—and certainly more attractive.

We are responsible for our own peace of mind. Staying angry, upset and bitter is certainly understandable in divorce. However, we don't have to cultivate or nurture these states that ultimately rob us of our beauty and serenity. We have better things to do.

One of the best ways to integrate what we've learned is to teach it. We listen, learn, practice, learn some more, fall back, learn, practice more and then teach. We can let people know that there is a better, happier route to follow. We have choices. We choose our attitudes. We can learn new ways. We can become healthier, smarter, more loving, and in turn, receive more good things.

This doesn't mean we should preach or tell people what to do. Remember Step One. After we've learned and practiced the first eleven steps, people will notice a change in us. Maybe we are more considerate, less volatile, less controlling, happier, more serene, able to listen without reacting, more generous, less worried, less harried and can admit when we're wrong. We attract new friends. Family or friends may ask why we're doing things differently. They may ask how and what we've learned. The door is open when people ask questions.

Example is the best teacher. "Walk the talk," as we say in the Twelve Step movement. Anyone can talk the talk—that's easy. Action is powerful and it is what people understand.

During a meeting, a man named Paul said that his wife, who had initiated the divorce, was miserable during their mediation process. Paul belonged to our Twelve Step

Step Divorce Group and was working hard on his own growth and adjustment to his current circumstances and newly defined responsibilities. She attacked and badgered him—probably out of her own fear. He told her that he wouldn't allow her to rob him of his hard-won serenity. She looked at him with a shocked expression, and said "*I* don't have any serenity! Why should *you* have serenity?" She didn't have the support that he had gotten for himself.

"Now she wants 50 percent of my serenity!" he announced at the meeting. This is when "carrying this message to others" becomes important. We say "If you want to be where I am, do what I did." You can't give serenity to someone else, nor can you demand or steal it. We earn it by letting go, practicing the Steps and taking one day at a time.

Always be open to new information. We are never too old to learn and grow, but we can't force what we've learned on anyone else.

The Twelfth Step asks us to continue to practice the Steps wherever they are applicable and to carry this message to others, whenever we are asked. Continued practice and sharing ideas with others keep us peaceful and in touch with the higher aspects of ourselves. Eventually with continued focus, the Steps create a global change in us, and our example inspires change in others.

Divorce induces transformation. Let's choose the best result possible. The unexpected benefit is that once we become more independent, whole and loving, we attract people who also have these characteristics.

Ideas for Working Step Twelve

When you get the concept of one of the Steps, teach it. Explain it to someone. Work it into a conversation. The more you explain it, the deeper the understanding becomes.

Start a meeting if there isn't one in your area. (See Chapter Four for guidance.) If you already attend a meeting, sign up to be a speaker. Be compassionate to someone who is going through a divorce.

Section Two

Tools for Recovery

Chapter Four

How to Create A Support Group

Because the concept of using the Twelve Steps to recover from divorce is not generally known, you may have to start your own group. Yes, there is work involved, but the rewards are worth the effort.

Specific suggestion about attracting membership and launching your group will come a bit later in this chapter, but first it's important to explore what is needed in a leader—the foundation of a successful group.

Deciding to Become a Leader

What are the characteristics you'll need? You'll need to:

♦ Have lived through separation or divorce.
♦ Have gone beyond the shock and pain of the initial separation.
♦ Like interaction with people.
♦ Have a sense of humor.
♦ Be able to speak about yourself to a number of people (usually six or so to begin with).
♦ Be there every week, or every other week—and on time. You can, of course, share the responsibility with another person or committee.

♦ Be responsible for use of a building with tasks like cleaning up and locking up. A committee is helpful here too.

♦ Be able to relate from your experience without getting caught up in it and forgetting that you're leading the meeting.

♦ Be strong enough not to date in the group, to avoid gossip and keep the confidentiality of group members.

♦ Have the humility to avoid judging others.

No one is perfect, but the success of a group depends on the reliability, integrity and maturity of its leaders. Leaders set the standard and create a safe place for people to share their feelings in a group setting.

Leadership Responsibilities

Twelve Step meetings are peer-led. No one takes on the role of therapist, and we refrain from giving direct personal advice at meetings. We aren't aware of anyone's "big picture" so what we say may cause more harm than good. Our job is simply to create a safe space for people to look at themselves and to encourage exploration.

How do we do that?

♦ Accept those who come to us with an open heart and mind. People at any level need to be accepted as they are. If you decide to lead a group, you will be amazed at the growth you will see in others and yourself. Pre-judging someone will cut off an avenue of mutual development. Keep an open mind about people and celebrate individuality.

♦ Refuse to gossip. Trust won't develop if group members think you'll talk about them when they aren't present.

♦ Be consistent with the meeting format. Folks who are going through separation and divorce have enough daily upheaval in their lives and feel better when they know what to expect. Routines create a feeling of safety.

♦ Remember names. It makes people feel welcome when they are greeted by name. This may take some practice, but it can be done.

♦ Realize that a group leader doesn't have to solve anyone's problems. A self-help group is just that—self-help. Your role is to listen and understand.

One way to give advice harmlessly is to have a resource table with helpful information, inspirational quotes and stories, and news about lectures and cultural events. Everyone may contribute to it. In other words, we can create a smorgasbord or buffet table where people can help themselves and choose the combination that is right for them, or feel free to choose nothing.

If asked for advice directly, speak from your own experience or from a story you know. Give your opinion with the preface "If *I* were in this circumstance, *I* would...." Or, "When that happened to me, this is what *I* did...." This gives a person something to think about without her feeling that she must follow the advice. "You should..." has an entirely different tone. As Ram Das says,

"You have to stop *shoulding* on yourself!" From experience I've learned that people take what they want and leave the rest. This is how we learn best—at our own pace, in our own time.

A visiting therapist commented on the sense of freedom she recognized in the group. The leader is free to interact with people without feeling responsible for everyone's problems, and the members are free to utilize what they need. No one is forcing or resisting. People are free to choose what suits them and will adapt it to their particular circumstances. This works really well.

On a personal note, I have led a group for the last five years, which has grown from six to 65 people. This has been one of the most rewarding experiences of my life. What goes around comes around, and my life has been blessed many times over.

A Twelve Step Recovery Meeting: Location

Find a central location to which you can give simple directions: a house of worship, community house, adult ed center, etc. Schedule an evening that's mutually convenient for both you and the facility. Try to conduct the meeting on neutral ground, rather than a private home. This way, if the leadership changes, it will not interfere with the meeting.

A support group for coping with divorce is a wonderful gift to the community. Most houses of worship are happy to lend space. Many churches and synagogues already have Twelve Step programs meeting in their buildings for other purposes.

Advertising

Advertise in local newspapers in the community announcements. Post fliers in libraries, supermarkets, post offices, etc. Give location, time, date and directions. Register with public agencies that refer people to services. For example:

> A Twelve Step Separation & Divorce Recovery Group will meet every Wednesday evening at 7:30 p.m. The meeting will be held at St. Mark's Episcopal Church, located at the junction of Routes 117 and 133 in Mt. Kisco. All are welcome. For further information, please call John Jones at 555-4321.

Be sure to return calls promptly.

Attracting Membership

It's helpful to begin with a few people you know. Ask friends who are going through or have been through the divorce experience to join you in starting a group. It's especially useful if there is someone who is or has been in a Twelve Step program.

Having both men and women in a group is very helpful to understand the two gender-perspectives of divorce. Men and women deal differently with some divorce issues, while some are experienced in the same way. It has been mentioned many times how good it is to hear the opposite sex's point of view from someone other than one's spouse. Having both sexes represented facilitates understanding and stops both male- and female-bashing, which isn't helpful and usually adds to the anger that we already feel. Neither men nor women want to walk into a group made up solely of the opposite sex—especially feeling as vulnerable as we do during divorce. Include both sexes in your beginning group, when possible.

Meeting Set-Up

Set chairs in a circle. Set up fewer chairs, rather than more. A lot of empty chairs look forlorn, but have more available. You'll get a feel for how many you need after a few weeks. Encourage latecomers to sit in the circle. Don't let anyone remain outside—it's distracting and seems to pull energy from the group.

Leading a Meeting

As we mentioned earlier, be consistent with the format. Confidence will grow when a participant feels comfortable and knows what to expect after attending a few meetings.

Be yourself. You are one of the members of this group and the more genuine you can be, the better. Just be sure that you don't monopolize the conversation. Everyone needs a chance to speak. Our meeting dwindled when one of our leaders couldn't stop talking about her own problems.

A critical part of the leader's job is to establish eye contact with the person who is speaking. Individuals tend to look at the leader most often when they are speaking. If the leader appears distracted or disinterested, the trust level goes down and the speaker becomes uncomfortable. The leader's body language is noticed, at least subconsciously. It's important to show by your posture that you are alert and interested in what is being said.

There will always be a variety of people at a meeting. You will like some right away and there will be those you won't like immediately. Some folks will be able to articulate what they think and some will struggle just to say a few words. Listen to everyone with an equal degree of respect, even if you greatly admire one and don't understand or appreciate another.

The Meeting Format

Begin the meeting with a moment of silence, because this stops conversations, calms the room and focuses the group into an introspective mood. Follow this with the Serenity Prayer.

Read the opening and the rules and then have everyone read the Steps together. People will at least hear them on a weekly basis.

You can adapt your own opening from my example below.

> The Opening:
> We welcome you to the Wednesday night meeting of the Twelve Step Separation - Divorce Recovery Group. [This meeting is sponsored by St. Mark's Episcopal Church, whose clergy and people also extend a warm welcome to you. [optional] We hope that by being together, by listening to each other, and by sharing our experience, strength and hope, we will learn to see the value of life in a new context.
>
> The purpose of this group is to establish a safe place where we can deal with the pain and isolation brought about by the ending of a significant relationship. We encourage and support those who want to make that ending as peaceful as possible.
>
> We encourage an atmosphere of connection and trust within the group, but we are not a singles group or a dating network. Instead, we are a family, where it is safe to be ourselves.
>
> The goal of this meeting is to help us develop into healthier, more complete,

independent, loving men and women. We grow by working on ourselves, and by letting go of the focus on others. This is done little by little, one day at a time.

Here are a few meeting rules:

1. What is said in this room is to be treated as confidential.

2. Everyone will have an opportunity to share.

3. You may pass, if you wish.

4. Please don't interrupt people who are speaking with either comments or questions. If you wish, speak to that person at the break or after the meeting.

5. Please keep your sharing within a five minute maximum. If you go over the allotted time, the meeting leader may interrupt you so that everyone has a chance to speak and the meeting doesn't run late.

We have chosen and adapted the Twelve Steps of Alcoholics Anonymous and Al-Anon as the basis of our recovery program because we know that this format works and that these principles have helped many people before us. The

Twelve Steps promote spirituality, not religion. Let's read the Steps together.

1.We admitted we were powerless over others—that our lives had become unmanageable.

2.Came to believe that a power greater than ourselves could restore us to wholeness.

3.Made a decision to turn our will and our lives over to the care of God, as we understood God.

4.Made a searching and fearless moral inventory of ourselves.

5.Admitted to God, to ourselves and to another human being the exact nature of our failings.

6.Were entirely ready to have God remove our defects of character.

7.Humbly asked God to remove our shortcomings.

8.Made a list of all persons we had harmed and became willing to make amends to them all.

9.Made direct amends to such people wherever possible, except when to do so would injure them or others.

10.Continued to take personal inventory and when we were wrong, promptly admitted it.

11.Sought through prayer and meditation to improve our conscious contact with God as we understood God, praying only for knowledge of His will for us and the power to carry that out.

12.Having had a spiritual awakening as a result of these Steps, we tried to carry this message to others and to practice these principles in all our affairs.

Start the discussion with an overview of why the Twelve Steps are an effective way to deal with divorce—something like...

We use the Twelve Steps because they have proven over the last 60 years to be useful in dealing with change. The Steps are best known in the field of recovery from addiction. Giving up an addiction means a change in priorities, relationships, social conditions, job status, sleep patterns and so on. The changes divorce precipitates are very similar. Through the use of the Steps, we are able to transform ourselves during this time of upheaval and change, and the changes we make now will alter our lives in ways that we can't even imagine. The Steps keep us focused on ourselves and the choices we make as we cope and adjust to our new situation. If we practice the Twelve Steps we will see that we heal, adjust and move on with hope, integrity, self-confidence and self-respect.

Then choose a step or slogan to talk about. As a leader, you will have to introduce the subject. If you have no experience with the Steps, read some material from this book aloud. There are many other resources to draw upon for new ideas on practicing the Steps. A bibliography has been placed at the back of this book for that purpose.

After your introduction, it works well to ask who wants to start the discussion. Work clockwise around the circle after the first speaker. People may pass if they wish. Use a hand signal of a T, or point to your watch to indicate to the speaker that his or her five-minute speaking time is up. If you plan to use this signal, let the group know in advance. If the group is small, timing isn't critical, although it's still important to keep things moving.

No Cross-Talk Allowed

Do not allow cross-talk, meaning side-conversations, argument or discussion of another person's point of view during the meeting. Everyone is entitled to discuss his or her own point of view only. At our group, we are given five minutes each to tell it as we see it without interruption or argument. When a person is finished, we say "Thanks, Mary." That's all. The meeting leader is not to argue with anyone. Cross-talk is strongly discouraged because a conversation can get started between two or three people, leaving the rest of the group uninvolved. This can escalate into an argument as well. The well-being of the group as a whole is our first responsibility. The best environment for a healthy group is a place where we are safe to speak our mind, without fear of argument or attack

It's amazing how much people grow and learn by using this format. We teach *ourselves* by working the Steps and by listening to others share their experience, strength and hope.

Refreshments

Refreshments are an important part of a meeting. Ideally we break from 8:45 to 9:00 which gives people a chance to talk in smaller groups or to ask some questions. Sharing food, however simple, unifies a group. Buy a supply of decaf coffee, sugar, stirrers, cups and cookies for the break.

Arrive early to set up and get the coffee going. I recommend decaf because divorcing people have enough trouble with sleepless nights. Refreshments are paid for from the money in the treasury.

Expenses

One or two dollars a week is collected from the membership to pay for the use of the building and for refreshments. We say, "We have no dues or fees, but we do have expenses."

Resource Table

We use a resource table to disseminate information not discussed in the meeting. This may include announcements of events, pertinent newspaper or magazine articles, handouts of uplifting sayings or quotes, phone lists and whatever else you feel may be of interest to your group. An additional option to consider is to offer books like this one and Melody Beattie's, *The Language of Letting Go*, for sale. We buy ten books at a time with money from the treasury, and then, as people buy them, we put the money back.

The Speaker

After the break we often have a group member tell his or her personal story. They share with others how they have coped and what they have learned so far. This is very effective because we hear people like ourselves tell of improvements they have made and we come to understand that we can make them too. A speaker talks for approximately 15 minutes about a subject related to divorce or self-improvement. Leave the last 15 minutes for questions.

We may arrange for guest speakers. Local professionals like therapists, mediators, psychologists, image consultants, and members of the clergy are often willing to speak to the group, free of charge, on a topic related to divorce. It's usually good for their practice or business, and the group gets the benefit of their point of view.

When thinking about possible speakers, ask for recommendations from your group. Over the years, we have invited divorce therapists, a family therapist, a child psychiatrist, mediators, a matrimonial attorney, an Episcopal priest who had been divorced, a Unitarian minister, an intuitive trainer, an image consultant, an acupuncturist, a person who sells related books, a group leader from a different area and a singles consultant.

At the time the appointment is made, advise the speaker that they need to teach the group something, not just do a commercial for their practice. Most professionals know this, but mentioning it makes it certain. Suggest that they bring a supply of handouts and business cards for anyone interested.

A Few Meetings Ideas

We try to keep a positive focus when selecting a topic. Subjects that help us get stronger, smarter, find peace, increase spirituality and find hope are prime. We think there is enough emphasis placed on legal and monetary issues everywhere else—so within our group we try to steer away from those topics.

Some ideas for possible meetings include:

◆ Discuss the Steps, which are the heart of the program. Take one a week and really try to understand it. They look simple but contain a great deal of wisdom and our perspective changes each time we discuss them.

◆ Use the slogans, which can be found in the Slogans and Quotes section of this book.

◆ There are many daily meditation books on the market. Use the reading of the day as a jumping-off place.

The Phone List

A list of first names and phone numbers is an important element in the life of a group. When he or she has a need to talk, a group member can find a sympathetic person to listen. Plans can be made and people can be contacted with meeting information, if necessary. I encourage the use of the phone list when feeling low, lonely or isolated.

Our group also has an e-mail list. Jokes, wisdom and notes of encouragement go back and forth all week. E-mail is a way to feel in touch with people in the middle of a sleepless night. E-mail addresses sometimes reveal last names or employer's names, so inform members of this prior to their participation on the list.

Suggestions For Success

Refrain From Judging

An important strength of a Twelve Step program is the wisdom that is present within the group. We are all at different stages of the divorce process and have had different experiences to bring us to our present circumstances. Listening to others is where we pick up ideas and stimulation to use in our own situation. It's interesting to note that wisdom often comes from the person we least expect to have anything helpful to say to us. Therefore it's important to refrain from judgment of one another.

Listen Attentively

Listening, rather than thinking only about what we intend to say, is a worthwhile habit to develop. Most of us can use the practice in attentive listening.

Speak From the "I" Perspective

Instead of saying "You dirty rat!" say "I am very angry!" This is a very effective communication technique. We get into trouble with name calling and pushing our state of mind onto someone else. On the other hand, we are entitled to feel the way we feel, and when we express this directly from our perspective, the other person can hear us. "I feel this way right now." There is no arguing with it.

When we attack a person, he or she will shut down and will be unable to hear us because of his or her defenses going up.

Suspend Disbelief

Many people have told stories about how they asked for help and, before long, an old friend calls. We see an article in the paper or magazine that gives us an idea or is relevant to what we need. We are in a hurry and all the traffic lights are green. The right therapist comes into our lives, etc. If we are alert, we will understand that our request has been answered. This is difficult to believe at first and requires practice and observation. Be willing to ask and stay alert.

Dating in the Group

Formula for Disaster
Man going through divorce + woman going through divorce + assorted children = emotional chaos.

The most controversial issue in the Separation/Divorce Recovery group is whether or not to date other group members. New people think dating should be allowed, but the more experienced people have seen what happens when dating occurs and choose not to become romantically involved with group members.

It requires a lot of time after a divorce to discover
who you are outside of that relationship. Take time
to increase awareness and avoid repeating history.

Divorce can be an important stage of growth and development. Because it's so painful, it is common to want to get through it and on to the next relationship as quickly as possible. Those of us who have been married a long time don't know how to be single. The last time we were unattached, we were younger, less experienced and had different needs. The quotes included in this chapter are taken from notes at a meeting where the topic was "Dating in the Group." The comments are from many different people.

The group provides a place where people in
recovery can communicate with and learn
to trust members of the opposite sex.

The ideal situation is to create a new social, but not romantic, avenue for ourselves. We need new friends—people to replace those who are now absent; those who will understand and empathize with the problems of divorce. We need company to go a movie, dinner, a concert or play—friends of the same sex and of the opposite sex. The group provides a sense of family. I've heard both men and women say that they've never had friends of the opposite sex before joining the group. For example, listening to men, women understand how difficult it is for fathers to be separated from their children. Listening to women, men hear the about the problems of being working moms with most of the parenting responsibility.

Earlier in this book we talked about impaired judgment while undergoing separation and divorce. We may be emotionally rocky and feel needy at times. This is no time to shop for a future mate. This is not to say that we can't connect with people and have fun. For many of us, the group becomes a second family of sisters and brothers, cousins, aunts and uncles. These relationships are all non-threatening and imply little obligation. We can do what we want, take advantage of opportunities that interest us, go home when we want—and relax! We aren't trying to be adorable and fabulous. We can take the time to find out what WE want. This is critical self-exploration that will help us know who we are in our new context as a single person.

> *The ability to speak freely and honestly*
> *without editing on any topic is very*
> *important.*

We have many important things to think about, and to dive into romance on the rebound will distract us from taking care of business. In a new relationship we are usually far too concerned about what the other person is thinking and feeling. If you are not divorced and are dating, this creates havoc. Any attorney will say that dating too early complicates the legalities.

If we have children, we need to be very thoughtful about the time a new romantic relationship will take away from them. Our children need stability more than usual during a divorce and having their parents involved elsewhere too soon creates more pain for them. They need time to adjust to their mom and dad living apart before they can accept another person. A romance demands a lot of energy and we find ourselves torn between the old relationship and the magnetism of the new.

Sorting out feelings in a new relationship is difficult. Achieving emotional clarity while going through a divorce, is almost impossible. It's much easier on all parties involved if we socialize with understanding friends rather than become emotionally embroiled.

Belonging to a divorce recovery group and attending meetings gives us the opportunity to listen to others and learn about what to do and not to do to make our lives easier and more peaceful. We share our experience, strength and hope with each other. We can be totally honest about ourselves and be accepted as we are. How often do we have the opportunity to spend two hours thinking about ourselves and our development? For many of us, the meeting is the only chance we'll have all week. It's an enormous relief to learn from the Steps and realize we are not alone. People have said that in the early stages of separation they lived from meeting to meeting. They couldn't wait to get back so they could feel normal and be reminded that, yes, they would survive.

When we date within the group, and sometimes that's very tempting, we alter that healing dynamic. We want to look good, sound smart and portray that we are farther along than we are. In other words, we put on a mask. The reality, especially in the beginning, is more likely that we still feel rejected and vulnerable, have trouble

slogans—all of which have aided in my growth and recovery.

One of the slogans that we have discussed many times is the "Attitude of Gratitude." This particular slogan has assisted in diminishing my anger toward my ex-spouse. To put it simply, I am thankful for the lessons I've learned with him, our memories, and most importantly, for our daughter.

The attitude of gratitude has begun to enter my consciousness lately, this being Thanksgiving. At the meetings we discuss making a list of ten things to be grateful for. On the Sunday evening before Thanksgiving, my seven-year-old daughter was feeling sad. As she lay in bed before going to sleep she began to express her pain regarding our divorce. I asked her to make a list of all the things she had to be thankful for. At first she did not want to let go of her anger. Then begrudgingly, she acknowledged being grateful for our dog. As we compiled her list together, her spirits lifted. Some of her answers surprised me, and I learned new things about her. She was excited when we finished. She couldn't believe she had twelve things and people to be thankful for!

I am grateful to have gained a tool, not only to use for myself when I am feeling down, but that I can also use to ease my child's pain in this process. There is a definite positive shift in our consciousness when we count our blessings!

FROM FRANK, December 1996

For me, the business of dealing with divorce has become a matter of "getting real" with myself. I have been forced to look at the foundations of not only my first marriage, but my second marriage as well.

I'm finding that this is a process of acknowledgment—of both the good and the bad. For years, without realizing it, I delighted in beating myself up emotionally and seeking the sympathy of the women in my life for things I thought I never got from my parents.

Mom and Dad, who are both gone now, did the best they could to raise my brother and me and give us all the love they could. As a younger person I allowed myself to feel cheated, and believed my brother was my father's favorite and I was my mother's favorite. Consequently I was looking to my first and second wives to be both mother and father to me. I wanted both their acceptance and rejection. My feeling was that in marriage, I would set things right in my life. I was looking to these women to provide for me the things, through no fault of their own, they were not able to provide for themselves.

Through my association with the Divorce Recovery Group and through therapy I am learning to discern between what *is* real and what I believed to be real.

The bottom line to all of this has been a realization that I don't blame the usual suspects—my mother, my father, my wives or myself. I realize that I have been operating from an incorrect definition of love. Now I am working on finding out what love is, starting with myself, by "getting real."

FROM ESTHER, July 1998

When I first walked into the Twelve Step Divorce and Separation Recovery Group, I was two years "down the road" from abandonment by my husband after 36 years of married life. I had been in therapy during that time and was continuing to try and work through my pain, grief and sometimes suicidal depression. My life felt at an end; I thought there could be nothing but despair and loneliness ahead of me.

The group changed all that. The Twelve Steps provided me with tools to work toward restoration of my emotional health. Not only did this occur, I came to see that there was some higher purpose in the painful process. I was, in this crisis, to uncover inner resources and find the person I was meant to be.

Left at age 58, now 63, I feel a whole new life *is* possible. This optimistic outlook is new for me, having spend most of my life thinking that I was not meant to be happy, that whenever something good happened, something bad was sure to follow. I have vowed that the last twenty-five percent of my life is going to be enjoyed, minute by minute, day by day without reference to the past and without focus on the future.

How has this transformation taken place?—slowly, over five year's time, and with much hard work. The Twelve Step group brought structure to this work. The Steps are designed to build one upon the next in a logical and life-enhancing way.

The first step—admitting that your life is unmanageable and that you have no control over the actions of others—was easy to embrace. It described where I was when I joined the group and defined the reality of the situation. Above all, it helped me to understand I was and could only be responsible for myself and no other. My obligation, as well, was to myself first and others second.

The second step—believing that a Higher Power could restore me to wholeness was an entirely different matter. I did not have faith enough to believe that "restoration" or "wholeness" was possible. I firmly believed that life would always conspire to keep me in the mire of depression. My sense of failure as a human being and wife was overwhelming. I felt helpless and a victim of circumstances beyond my control. I was stuck on Step 2.

It was not until four years had passed and I was growing tired and impatient with my position in the "mud," that I met with Micki McWade, the group leader, for breakfast on a Sunday morning. She suggested that I go home and write out the following: What I wanted to do. What would happen if I didn't do it. What strategies I would use to accomplish what I wanted done. When I got home I made a sign and taped it on my kitchen door. It read: I want to get out of the mud. If I don't, I will self-destruct. The strategy: "act as if" and pray.

The real work began; I had finally decided to abandon the role of victim and become proactive—an advocate of myself. Setting the goal, employing strategies of "acting as if I was the person I wanted to be" and praying mightily began to pay off. I did feel better, I looked better, and good things began happening.

The move from Step Two to Step Three was part of the prayer process. For in acknowledging that I had been unable to effect change on my own, I embraced as often as

I could the idea that God had a plan for me and that I could trust his good judgment. Thus, in "turning it over" I was allowing myself to relax and go with the flow. This has not proven an easy task, for often I take back what I've given over or let go. Despite a less-than-perfect score on this third Step, I do believe this is a key to freeing the mind and soul from the burden of fear about the future.

These three steps form the foundation for the remaining nine that deal with self-evaluation and restructuring one's emotional life and person-to-person relationships. To accept that the work of self-discovery is never done is to continue to grow throughout life—and the Twelve Steps are there as guideposts.

FROM EDDIE, July 1998
ON STEP 1

I definitely believe that each moment is a gift from God that comes and goes in the blink of an eye. I guess a good moral here is "seize the moment," and enjoy it before it goes by. Too many times we get caught up and worried about what's happening. Thanks to the group meetings and practicing the Twelve Steps, I have changed my whole attitude and way of thinking. When something negative or that I would normally get worried sick about happens, my new attitude is "I am POWERLESS and have no control over this," and then I flip the coin over and ask myself "How can I turn this negative situation into something positive?" To some it may sound corny, but when I'm in a negative situation, I now always ask myself "What would God want me to do here?" and I then ask for guidance.

This usually leads me on a positive path with the next step I take.

Speaking of a gift from God, I thought a lot about my personal situation and the negative things my wife has said and done which, in the past, would have caused me to become irate, upset, and react in a negative manner. One day it occurred to me that this goes against what I teach my kids: "Two wrongs don't make a right," and "If he jumped off a bridge, would you?" So now I do what I think is right because I strongly believe that it's God's way, and in the end, when it's time to face the music, we all have to take responsibility for our actions and behavior.

On Step 3

I really do try to turn the uncontrollable stuff over to God. Many times I feel at ease after doing so, which is an indicator to me that I did the right thing. I guess part of me wonders if I am just blocking things out or if I'm truly turning them over. I'm not used to being able to let things go so easily without having my blood pressure rise and having my stomach turn at 2000 revolutions per second. It doesn't feel normal; but then again, the feeling of being at peace because of turning things over eliminates all of those negative side effects. I guess the way I look at it now is that I can't worry about whether I am blocking things out or turning them over. If I am blocking them, they will hit me in the face again and I will have another opportunity to deal with them. If they don't return, I'll know that I have successfully turned them over.

After all, I have a life to start living again and I can't control what I can't control—no matter how hard I try.

ON STEP 4

As we discussed last night, we have our highs and lows
.This week has been kind of low, but I'm trying the best I
can to get myself back up. As I mentioned last night, I
signed the separation/divorce papers before coming to the
meeting. Thank God I had the meeting to go to afterwards!

Today I attended my younger son's school music festi-
val. My wife and her mother also came. This was the first
time I saw her mother since this whole separation/divorce
thing started. It was strange.

I arrived at the school first and my wife and her mom
were about an hour late. I saved two seats for them, which
was good because there was only standing room by time
they arrived. I waved them down when I saw them standing in the corner. I also made the first move to give my
soon-to-be ex-mother-in-law a kiss hello, which I can tell
you *she* wasn't about to do. I didn't have to save the seats
or make the first move with the greeting, but again I
thought it was the right thing to do. Sometimes doing the
little things right helps to give me confidence that I can do
the right thing when faced with the biggies.

FROM ROBERT, December 1996

It is Wednesday evening. The time is 7:30; and unless
some personal emergency arises, I will settle into a seat at
my divorce support group. The chairs have been set in a
circle, ready to accommodate me and the twenty-five to
thirty other people who value this group as a form of life
support.

I am relatively new to this group and have not yet bought into the entire program as I continue to evaluate and reflect on what it offers me, as well as what contribution I can make to others. My initial experience, about three months ago, was colored with curiosity, apprehension and cynicism. However, I walked out at the end of that first meeting knowing I would return the following week. I felt warmly accepted as I listened carefully to the very heart warming, amusing and supportive stories shared by those in our circle. I was very impressed by the many highly intelligent and articulate people sitting with me.

I do have a problem with the reference to God or any higher power that has influence over my life. Although the Twelve Step model has a proven track record, I'm not sure if it's for me. My primary focus is on utilizing my strengths to grow beyond the self-imposed restrictions that keep me from enjoying life. So far, it appears that my ideas and the Twelve Steps can coexist. With all that being said, I very much value the people who come every week to share, weep and celebrate.

I need this group as a building block toward more social interaction. I spend too much time alone. The group phone list rests in my drawer waiting for me to reach out. Learning to ask for help is an important priority. There are specific men's issues that I want to discuss with my fellow gender travelers. The landscape for men and women has some unique terrain. There are several men whose sharing touches chords that resonate strongly within me. I am working toward calling these members and making time to be together outside of the group. I must admit I have reservations about relating to members in a social situation. It is something I will have to give myself a chance to experience. Friendship has always been the greatest comfort in my existential loneliness.

I recently brought up the fact that sex is a topic that is never raised in our discussions. If we are to do better in our next relationships I believe that we must understand the power and beauty of sexual intimacy. Our group leader challenged me to lead a discussion on this subject from whatever angle I felt comfortable with. I was very impressed with her ability to confront my concern as well as getting me actively involved. Obviously the issues of sex in our recovery cannot be underestimated or denied.

For now I have decided to be an active and supportive member. I am hopeful that our divorce group will help me reach a stage where I am ready to be more engaged and capable of making those life choices that will keep me *alive*. Soon I will test the waters to discover if I am ready to trust and love another. All these recovery steps will become possible, as I learn from the group members who share their journeys with me every Wednesday night at 7:30.

FROM MIKE, December 1996

I began attending the weekly meetings of the Separation/Divorce Recovery Group about one and a half years ago, within a month of splitting up with my second wife, and I believe that the group and its philosophical approach have been major factors in my recovery from this experience and the continuing maintenance of my emotional well-being.

The message of the Serenity Prayer and the concept of letting go, a recognition of the limitations of our abilities to control and influence situations, are directly opposed to the confrontational, adversarial approach that we so easily fall into in a divorce situation. The focus on healing ourselves through group interaction, and not on negative judgmental attitudes toward our estranged spouses, is a positive approach to recovery, as opposed to vindictiveness and getting even.

The group dynamic has worked for me in two ways; it first provided a receptive sympathetic forum for expressing my thoughts and feelings, and secondly, my listening to the experiences and perspectives of others in similar situations gave me more insight into my own situation. Since we have all had the separation/divorce experience in common, in many ways it is easier and less inhibiting for us to speak to the group than to family and friends who also knew our estranged spouses and may be judgmental toward us.

The group also serves as a social circle for those of us who are suddenly isolated from previous friends as a result of a separation, in which frequently it is only one of the two estranged parties that stays within the social network that they both were previously involved in as a couple. Since we participate in non-meeting social activities as a group, it is psychologically easier for those of us who are not yet emotionally ready to re-enter the singles dating scene.

The core of the Twelve Step program is our recognition that we cannot get through this difficult period alone, and that we need the help of a higher power to aid our recovery. Although the Steps refer to God, as we understood God, for those of us without a strong religious background the higher power becomes the group itself, and the weekly meetings a form of symbolic worship service. I have found the Steps and the additional slogans and proverbs to be very helpful in my continuing journey through the difficult passage of life.

FROM LAURIE, August 1998

The Step that has helped me the most is Step One: *We admitted that we were powerless over others that our lives had become unmanageable.*

The "powerlessness over others" part has freed me from always trying to please others and get them to like me and has turned the focus onto pleasing and liking myself. The flipside to "powerlessness over others" is powerful over ourselves and this concept has been the key to my recovery. Instead of expecting others to take care of me, I realize that I have to take responsibility for myself if I am to become a complete and fully developing adult. My life is in my own hands and I am capable, and actually the most qualified, of making my life full and rich and meaningful. My focus is on me. When my life starts to get out of balance, I literally ask myself "What is best for me? How can I take care of myself?" I try to do what is best, even if it means doing some things I don't really like to do or that I'm afraid to do.

Step One has also been invaluable in figuring out my contribution to the breakdown of our marriage. It is a lot easier to blame my husband than to accept some responsibility for myself, but the knowledge I have gained is truly a gift. I know myself on a deeper level and hopefully that will help me to have more meaningful and loving relationships in the future.

This is an ongoing process. We are all works in progress.

FROM KAREN, May 1998

I can't tell you how many times I have returned home on a Wednesday night, strengthened by the discussions the group has had. They go a long way to making me feel whole again and that helps me deal with the everyday family issues in a much stronger way. Last night, for example, I felt so much better when I got home that I was able to discuss an issue with my 19 year old daughter that both of us had felt badly about. Good communication is always the key and we discussed how each other felt about what had happened. Sometimes we're just so mad we can't do that. I am sorely missing the support and love of another adult in my life and it feels so much better to talk about the divorce issues and hear from people who understand what it's like. It's the best and thanks so much.

Conclusion

I'd like to share an observation. In the ten years of Twelve Step meetings I've been privileged to attend I've noticed that there are three general types of meeting attendees. Some come to one or two meetings and don't come back. This is natural—everyone will not follow the same path. Some come for the social interaction, which is natural too. Twelve Step people are usually friendly, warm and accepting. The meetings provide a vehicle to make new friends and foster a feeling of inclusion. I'm sure you know that while going through a divorce, acceptance is very important. There are people who understand the merits of the Steps intellectually and agree with them, but they stop there. They don't actually practice them.

Then there are the people who not only like the social interaction and understand the Steps, they *practice* them and integrate them into their lives. These are the people who gain the deepest understanding and make sweeping changes in their thinking. They move on from divorce and out of the patterns that were causing them difficulty into a life of proactive choice and achieving serenity a lot of the time. I use the word *achieve* because serenity, or the state of peace, during or after separation and divorce is not easy to come by. It's a state that's earned.

There is no judgment implied by these statements. Everyone is welcome to participate to the degree they wish. This is written only to encourage you to realize your potential for transformation by practicing the Twelve Steps during this difficult time.

I wish you the best in your recovery. I am well-acquainted with the pain you may be in right now and I guarantee that it will lessen in time. Make the most of this period, and take it one day at a time.

Blessings,

Micki McWade

Resources

A Course In Miracles. Triburon, CA: Foundation for Inner Peace, 1975.
A modern interpretation of the psychological and spiritual aspects of the teachings of Jesus Christ, with particular emphasis on forgiveness.

Bach, Richard. *Illusions: The Adventures of a Reluctant Messiah.* New York: Dell, 1977.
An inspirational story about a pilot meeting a miraculous man who was also a pilot and healer.

Beattie, Melody. *The Language of Letting Go.* New York: Harper Collins, 1990.
Daily meditations to create autonomy and to ease pain in relationships, with a Twelve Step focus.

Campbell, Joseph, Bill Moyers. *The Power of the Myth.* New York: Bantam Books, 1991.
A transcript of a television interview. An explanation of how the god/goddess archetypes influence the personality.

Covey, Stephen R. *The Seven Habits of Highly Effective People.* New York: Fireside Books, Simon and Schuster, 1990.
Description of a thought system that teaches ways to improve life by defining life goals within the context of the

various roles that make up our personality and areas of responsibility.

Hahn, Thich Nhat. *Peace is Every Step: The Path of Mindfulness in Everyday Life*. New York: 1991.
Essays on how to enhance consciousness in the ordinary activities of life.

Hay, Louise. *You Can Heal Your Life*. Santa Monica, CA: Hay House, 1984.
Suggests that physical ailments are connected to the belief systems of the mind. Once beliefs are understood they can be changed and symptoms stop.

Kabat-Zinn. *Wherever You Go, There You Are, Mindful Meditation in Everyday Life*.

L'Engle, Madeleine. *Two Part Invention*. New York: Harper & Row, 1989.
A description of a marriage and what makes it work.

Oliver-Diaz, Philip and Patricia A. O'Gorman. *12 Steps to Self-Parenting*. Deerfield Beach, FL: Health Communications, 1984.
Suggestions for giving ourselves what we may have missed as children.

Rodegast, Pat and Judith Stanton. *Emmanuel's Book*. New York: Bantam Books, 1987.
Transcript of questions and answers about life between a channeled entity and a group of students.

Walsch, Neale Diamond. *Coversations with God: An Uncommon Dialogue.*

Williamson, Marianne. *Illuminata.* New York: Random House, 1994.
A collection of thoughts, prayers and ceremonies.

Index

A

A Course in Miracles, 73
AA, 3, 12
act as if, 62
admitting, 50
Al-Anon, 3, 9, 12
alcoholism, 12, 14
amputation, 5
anger, 83
apology, 73–74
ask/listen, 78
asking and receiving, 59
attitude, 125, 141
attorneys, 22, 72
awful-izing, 9

B

Bach, Richard, 57, 122
beginners mind, 60–61
bliss, 77

C

came to believe, 30
Campbell, Joseph, 77
carrying the message, 82
characteristics list, 41–42
choices, 24
choosing reactions, 14
civility, 36
communication, 69
conscious contact, 77

continuous apology, 73
continuous inventory, 73
control, 35
Covey, Stephen R., 4, 6

D

Dating, 105–115
dealing with change, 15, 37, 59
denial, 50, 54

E

email list, 103
emotional/legal definitions, 71
environment, creating my, 70
ex-spouse relationship, 36
eye-contact, 94

F

faith, 33
family events, 36
fault, 65
finding our place, 78
Frankl, Viktor, 24

G

gateway, 4, 37
getting answers, 32
giving advice, 90
God Can, 38

S

self-exploration, 39, 147
serenity, 8, 37
Shakespeare, William, 62
shortcoming replacement list, 55–56
shortcomings, 40, 56, 59
smoking example, 54–55
speeding example, 54
spiritual awakening, 82
stages of divorce, 23
Step 1, 22–27, 145, 151
Step 2, 28–32
Step 3, 33–38, 146
Step 4, 39–49, 147
Step 5, 50–53
Step 6, 54–58
Step 7, 59–63
Step 8, 64–67
Step 9, 68–72
Step 10, 73–75
Step 11, 76–81, 137
Step 12, 82–85
Steps overview, 98–99
Steps—interpretation, 76
strengths, 40
support group, 3, 4
support, 51

T

talking to God, 34
teaching, 83
time formula, 29
tools, 6
trauma, 1, 5

turning it over, 33, 37
Twelve Step Meetings, 9
Twelve Steps and addiction, 14
Twelve Steps of AA, 16
Twelve Steps of Divorce Recovery, 18

V

vicious cycle, 69

W

walking the talk, 83
wholeness, 28
Williamson, Marianne—prayer, 25

Support Groups

If you decide to start a support group, please contact Micki McWade with details. She will be happy to refer people to your group if asked for a referral in your area.

If you have questions about starting a group, e-mail Micki McWade at

mmcwade@bestweb.net

Web Site

Visit the web site of
Getting Up, Getting Over and Getting On at:
http://www.12stepdivorce.org
For book news and author appearances visit the
Champion Press, Ltd. web site at:
http://www.championpress.com

About the Author

When Micki was separated in 1990, she had been married for twenty-three years and had four adolescent children. Many people said "You'd better get a good lawyer and get ready to fight." By that time, she had been a member of Al-Anon and had been practicing the Twelve Steps for five years and she knew there was a better way. She used this gentle philosophy to guide her through her separation and divorce and realized how helpful the Steps could be in creating a feeling of serenity—a commodity in short supply during divorce.

Micki McWade is a graphic artist and writer, a mother of four grown children, and married to her second husband, Gary Ditlow. She lives in New York.

Author Availability

Micki McWade is available for conferences, workshops and instruction on Twelve Step Divorce Recovery. For more information on these opportunities or to contact the author, write to:

Micki McWade
Post Office Box 453
Garrison, NY 10524

Discounts

Quantity discounts are available on this title. For more information contact Champion Press at 264 S. La Ceienega Blvd., Suite 1064; Beverly Hills, CA 90211.

TATIANA

a novel

Where do you go when no place is safe?

What appears at first to be a simple accident soon becomes a web of deadly agendas when a young woman captures on videotape the horrific crash of an airliner into the deserted Dutch countryside. News accounts detail the final moments of Moscow Air 119, but when they're drastically different than what Tatiana's camera recorded, she fights to make her tape public and is immediately fighting for her very life. When no place is safe, Tatiana turns to the one person she has always counted on...herself.

by Greg Anderson
$22.95, Hardcover, ISBN 1-891400-40-1

Back to Basics

101 Ideas for Strengthening Our Children And Our Families

by Brook Noel
ISBN: 1-891400-48-7
$13.95

I Wasn't Ready to Say Good Bye
A Guide To Coping, Surviving and Healing After Tragic Loss

by Pamela D. Blair, Ph.D. and Brook Noel
ISBN: 1-891400-27-4
October, 1999.

---

365 Easy, Quick and Inexpensive Dinner Menus that Even The Kids Will Love!

by Penny E. Stone
ISBN: 1-891400-33-9
December, 1999.

Choosing Simplicity:

Restoring Joy and Sanity to
Bankrupt Lives

by Deborah Taylor-Hough
ISBN: 1-891400-49-5
November, 1999.

If you would like a catalog of
titles by Champion Press,
send your request to the address below.

Quantity discounts are available
on all Champion titles.
write to Champion press for more information.

Champion Press, Ltd.
264 South La Cienega Blvd., Suite 1064
Beverly Hills, CA 90211

EDUCATIONAL AND GROUP DISCOUNTS ARE AVAIL-
ABLE FOR MORE INFORMATION WRITE TO CHAMPION
PRESS, LTD.

Please photocopy this page to order additional titles by Champion
Press, Ltd. Or on-line at our web site, www.championpress.com.

QUANTITY   TITLE   PRICE

_____   _____   _____
_____   _____   _____
_____   _____   _____
_____   _____   _____
_____   _____   _____
_____   _____   _____
_____   _____   _____

_____ Shipping and handling. $3.95 for the first book and $1
more for each additional book
_____ Payment enclosed
_____ Please charge my ___ Visa ___ MasterCard

Account Number _____

Expiration Date _____

Signature _____

Name as it appears on card _____

Name _____

Address _____

City _____ State _____ Zip _____

Day Phone _____

Autograph Copy Yes ____ No ____

MAIL FORM TO:

Champion Press, Ltd.

264 S. La Cienega Blvd., Suite 1064

Beverly Hills, CA 90211